SECOND EDITION

WORD DIVISION MANUAL

THE FIFTEEN THOUSAND MOST-USED WORDS IN BUSINESS COMMUNICATION

J. E. SILVERTHORN
Formerly of Oklahoma State University

and

DEVERN J. PERRY
Brigham Young University

K48   SOUTH-WESTERN PUBLISHING CO.

Cincinnati, OH 45227   Chicago, IL 60644   Dallas, TX 75229
Burlingame, CA 94010   New Rochelle, NY 10802

FOREWORD

WORD DIVISION MANUAL, Second Edition, contains 15,659 words, arranged alphabetically, illustrating acceptable and preferred points at which these words may be divided. The words selected for inclusion in this Manual come from two extensive tabulations of words used in approximately 4,100 pieces of business communications, as identified by two doctoral studies: "The Basic Vocabulary of Written Business Communications," by James Edwin Silverthorn, completed in 1956 at Indiana University; and "An Analytical Comparison of the Relative Word-Combination Frequencies of Business Correspondence with Phrase Frequencies of Selected Shorthand Textbooks," by Devern J. Perry, completed in 1968 at the University of North Dakota.

All words appearing in the 4,100 business letters, regardless of frequency, were tabulated in the studies. From this extensive tabulation, words representing individual, company, and brand names were excluded as were capitalized words and abbreviations. Thus this Manual contains the pure basic vocabulary of the business communications sampled for these studies.

In order to increase the usefulness of this book as a source of reference for spelling and word division, some words in addition to those encountered in the Silverthorn-Perry tabulation have been included. Only those words that might cause spelling and/or division difficulties and that might occur in business writing were added. All these words appeared in the general vocabulary tabulation of Kučera-Francis (Henry Kučera and W. Nelson Francis, *Computational Analysis of Present-Day American English*). For ease of identification, these words have been preceded by asterisks.

The user of this Manual will note that word division is indicated by both a hyphen and a period. Recommended points at which words may be divided at the ends of lines are shown by a hyphen; for example, *bril-liant*. Acceptable, but not preferred, division points according to the rules for division contained within this Manual are indicated by a period; for example, *ef·fort*.

v

Although some words may be acceptably divided at any one of several points, readability suggests one or two points of division that are preferable. Examples showing preferred division points are *in·gre-di·ents* and *pos·si-bil·ity*.

A boldface hyphen is used to indicate that a compound word written in hyphenated form may be acceptably divided only at the point of the existing hyphen; for example, *above‑mentioned*.

Webster's Third New International Dictionary, unabridged, was used as the authority for spelling and syllabication in this Manual.

GUIDELINES FOR WORD DIVISION

An extensive examination of word division rules revealed that the guidelines presented below are widely accepted. These guidelines, therefore, were followed in the preparation of this edition of the WORD DIVISION MANUAL.

1. Although the most desirable point at which to divide a word is sometimes a matter of opinion, it is preferable to have enough of the word on the first line to give the reader the concept of the entire word, and to carry enough of the word to the next line to have two significantly sized parts. Pronunciation of the word is also an important factor to consider in determining the best division point.

2. Words should be divided only between syllables. One-syllable words, such as *shipped*, *course*, and *league*, must not be divided.

3. There must be more than one letter with the first part of the word (*im-port*, but not i-deals); and more than two letters with the last part of the word (*hur-ried*, but not speak-er).

Even though such divisions are acceptable, it is desirable to avoid setting off two letters at the beginning of a word. These are acceptable but not preferred divisions and are indicated by a period rather than a hyphen; for example, *in·creas-ing*.

4. Even though they may have two or more syllables, never divide words of five or fewer letters, such as *other* and *idea*. If possible, avoid dividing words of six letters; for example: *letter* is better than *let-ter*.

5. When a final consonant, preceded by a single vowel, is doubled before adding a suffix, divide between the two consonants; for example, *let·ting*, not lett-ing. However, when a root word ends in a double consonant before a suffix is added, divide between the root word and the suffix; for example, *bill-ing*, not bil-ling.

6. Compound words written without the hyphen are preferably divided between the elements of the compound, such as *business-men*, not businessmen. Compound words written with the hyphen should be divided only at the point of the existing hyphen, such as *self-addressed*.

7. A single-letter syllable within a word should be written with the first part of the word, such as *tabu-late*, not tab-ulate.

Exceptions:

When a word ends in a two-letter syllable preceded by a single-vowel syllable, the two ending syllables may be joined and carried over to the next line (*hast-ily*).

When the single-letter syllable *a*, *i*, or *u* is followed by the ending syllable *ble*, *bly*, *cle*, or *cal*, the two ending syllables should be joined when carried over to the next line (*cur-able*, *favor-ably*, *mir-acle*, *cler-ical*).

When two one-letter syllables occur together within a word, divide between the one-letter syllables (*evalu-ation*).

8. When it is necessary to divide parts of a date, a proper name, or an address, divide at the logical point for readability.

Divide between the day of the month and the year (*March 13,-1969*), not between the month and the day (March-13, 1969).

Divide between parts of the name as illustrated: *Mr. Jack-Jones*, not Mr.-Jack Jones; *Thomas-Brown, M.D.*, not Thomas Brown-M.D.

Divide the address between the city and the state (*Cincinnati,-Ohio 45227*), not between the state and the zip code (Cincinnati, Ohio-45227).

9. Avoid dividing figures, abbreviations, and signs representing words or abbreviations. (*$10,000*, not $10,-000 nor $-10,000; *A.T.&T.*, not A.T.-&T.; *#57*, not #-57; and *30 ft.*, not 30-ft.)

10. Avoid dividing the last word of more than two consecutive lines. Also avoid dividing the last word of a paragraph or the last word of a page.

11. When determining the points at which to end a line, it should be remembered that how the line ends has considerable influence on the degree of ease with which the reader can follow the thought of the written expression. Therefore, the division of words should be minimized; and when the separation of related items is necessary, the break should be a logical one.

a
aban-don
aban-doned
aban-don-ment
abbey

*ab-bre-via-ted
ab-bre-via-tions
abey-ance
abide
abili-ties

abil-ity
able
ably
ab-nor-mal
ab-nor-mali-ties

ab-nor-mally
aboard
abomi-na-ble
about
above

above-mentioned
abra-sion
abra-sions
abra-sive
abra-sives

abreast
abroad
abrupt
ab-sence
ab-sent

ab-sen-tee
ab-sen-tee-ism
ab-sent-ing
ab-so-lute
ab-so-lutely

ab-sorb
ab-sorbed
ab-sor-bent
ab-sorb-ing
ab-sorp-tion

ab-stain-ers
ab-stract
ab-strac-tor
ab-strac-tors
ab-stracts

*ab-surd
abun-dance
abun-dant
abut
abut-ting

aca-deme
aca-demic
aca-demi-cally
acad-emy
ac-ceded

ac-ced-ing
ac-cel-er-ate
ac-cel-er-ated
ac-cel-er-at-ing
ac-cel-era-tion

ac-cent
ac-cen-tu-ated
ac-cept
ac-cepta-bil-ity
ac-cept-able

ac-cep-tance
ac-cep-tances
ac-cepted
ac-cept-ing
ac-cepts

ac-cess
ac-ces-si-ble
ac-ces-sion
ac-ces-so-rial
ac-ces-so-ries

ac-ces-sory
ac-ci-dent
ac-ci-den-tal
ac-ci-den-tally
ac-ci-dents

ac-claim
ac-claimed
ac-com-mo-date
ac-com-mo-dated
ac-com-mo-dat-ing

ac-com-mo-da-tion
ac-com-mo-da-tions
ac-com-pa-nied
ac-com-pa-nies
ac-com-pany

ac-com-pa-ny-ing
*ac-com-plice
ac-com-plish
ac-com-plished
ac-com-plishes

ac-com-plish-ing
ac-com-plish-ment
ac-com-plish-ments
ac-cord
ac-cor-dance

ac-corded
ac-cord-ing
ac-cord-ingly
ac-cor-di-ons
ac-count

ac·coun·tancy
ac·coun·tant
ac·coun·tants
ac·counted
ac·count·ing

ac·counts
ac·credi·ta·tion
ac·cred·ited
ac·crual
ac·crue

ac·crued
ac·crues
ac·cru·ing
ac·cu·mu·late
ac·cu·mu·lated

ac·cu·mu·la·tion
ac·cu·mu·la·tions
ac·cu·mu·la·tive
ac·cu·racy
ac·cu·rate

ac·cu·rately
ac·cu·sa·tion
ac·cuse
ac·cus·tomed
ace

ace·tate
achieve
achieved
achieve·ment
achieve·ments

achiev·ing
acid
acids
ac·knowl·edge
ac·knowl·edged

ac·knowl·edges
ac·knowl·edg·ing
ac·knowl·edg·ment
ac·knowl·edg·ments
*acous·tic

acous·ti·cal
ac·quaint
ac·quaint·ance
ac·quaint·ance·ship
ac·quainted

ac·quaint·ing
ac·quaints
ac·quire
ac·quired
ac·quires

ac·quir·ing
ac·qui·si·tion
ac·qui·si·tions
ac·quit·tance
*ac·quit·ted

acre
acre·age
acre·ages
acres
ac·ri·lan

ac·ro·nym
across
acrylic
act
acted

act·ing
ac·tion
ac·tions
ac·ti·va·ted
ac·ti·vates

ac·tive
ac·tively
ac·tivi·ties
ac·tiv·ity
actor

acts
ac·tual
ac·tu·ally
ac·tu·arial
ac·tu·ar·ies

ac·tu·ary
ac·tua·ted
acute
acutely
ad

ad va·lo·rem
adage
adapt
adapta·bil·ity
adapt·able

ad·ap·ta·tion
adapted
adapt·ing
add
added

ad·den·dum
add·ing
ad·di·tion
ad·di·tional
ad·di·tion·ally

ad·di·tions
ad·dress
ad·dressed
ad·dressee
ad·dresser

ad·dress-ers
ad·dresses
ad·dress-ing
adds
ade

ade-noid
ade-noids
*adept
ade-quacy
ade-quate

ade-quately
ad·here
ad·hered
ad·her-ence
ad·her-ent

ad·heres
ad·he-sion
ad·he-sive
ad·ja-cent
ad·join-ing

ad·journ
ad·journed
ad·journ-ing
ad·journ-ment
ad·judged

ad·ju-di-ca-tion
ad·ju-di-ca-tory
ad·juncts
ad·just
ad·just-able

ad·justed
ad·juster
ad·just-ers
ad·just-ing
ad·just-ment

ad·just-ments
ad·min-is-ter
ad·min-is-tered
ad·min-is-ter·ing
ad·min-is-ters

ad·min-is-tra-tion
ad·min-is-tra-tions
ad·min-is-tra-tive
ad·min-is-tra·tor
ad·min-is-tra·tors

ad·mi-ra·ble
ad·mi-ral
ad·mi-ra-tion
ad·mire
ad·mis-sion

ad·mis-sions
admit
ad·mit-tance
ad·mit-ted
ad·mit-tedly

ad·mit-ting
ad·mix-ture
ad·mo-ni-tion
ado-les-cent
ado-les-cents

adopt
adopted
adopt-ing
adop-tion
ads

adult
adults
ad·vance
ad·vanced
ad·vance-ment

ad·vances
ad·vanc-ing
ad·van-tage
ad·van-ta-geous
ad·van-tages

ad·vent
ad·verse
ad·versely
ad·ver-sity
ad·ver-tise

ad·ver-tised
ad·ver-tise-ment
ad·ver-tise-ments
ad·ver-tiser
ad·ver-tis·ers

ad·ver-tises
ad·ver-tis·ing
ad·vice
ad·vices
ad·visa-bil·ity

ad·vis-able
ad·vise
ad·vised
ad·vise-ment
ad·viser

ad·vis-ers
ad·vises
ad·vis-ing
ad·vi-sor
ad·vi-sors

ad·vi-sory
ad·vo-cate
ad·vo-cates
aegis
aera-ting

ae·rial, adj.
aer·ial, n.
aero-com-mander
aero-bic
aero-nau-ti·cal

aero-nau-tics
aero-sol
aero-space
*aes-thetic
af·fair

af·fairs
af·fect
af·fected
af·fect-ing
af·fec-tion

af·fec-tions
af·fects
af·fi-da·vit
af·fi-da·vits
af·fili-ate

af·fili-ated
af·fili-ates
af·fili-ation
af·fir-ma-tions
af·fir-ma-tive

af·fir-ma-tively
af·firmed
affix
af·fixed
af·fix-ing

af·flu-ence
af·ford
af·forded
af·fords
afoot

afore-men·tioned
afore-said
afoul
afraid
after

af·ter-noon
af·ter-noons
af·ter-wards
again
against

ag·ates
age
aged
agen-cies
agency

agenda
agent
agents
ages
*ag·gra-vate

ag·gra-va-tion
ag·gre-gate
ag·gre-gat·ing
ag·gres-sion
ag·gres-sive

ag·gres-sors
ago
agony
agree
agree-able

agree-ably
agreed
agree-ing
agree-ment
agree-ments

agrees
agri-busi-ness
ag·ri-cul-tural
ag·ri-cul-tur-al-ists
ag·ri-cul-tur-ally

ag·ri-cul-ture
agrono-mist
agron-omy
ahead
aid

aide
aided
aide-de-camp
aides
aid·ing

aids
ail·ing
ail-ments
aim
aimed

aim·ing
aims
air
air-conditioned
air-conditioning

air-craft
aired
air-lift
air-line
air-lines

air-mail
air-mailed
air-mail·ing
air-park
air-plane

air-planes
air-port
air-show
air-ways
aisle

alarm
alarm-ing
alarm-ingly
album
al·bums

al·co-hol
al·co-holic
alert
alerted
alerts

al·falfa
al·ge-bra
alibi
alien
alien-at·ing

aligned
align-ments
aligns
alike
*ali-mony

alive
al·kali
al·ka-lies
al·ka-line
all

al·le-ga-tions
*al·lege
al·leged
al·leges
*al·le-giance

al·ler-gic
al·ler-gies
al·le-vi·ate
al·le-vi-ated
al·le-via-ting

al·lied
al·lo-cate
al·lo-cated
al·lo-cates
al·lo-ca-ting

al·lo-ca-tion
al·lo-ca-tions
allot
al·lot-ment
al·lot-ments

al·lot-ted
all-out
allow
al·low-able
al·low-ance

al·low-ances
al·lowed
al·low-ing
al·lows
alloy

al·ma-nac
al·most
alone
along
along-side

aloof
alpha
al·pha-betic
al·pha-beti-cally
al·pine

al·ready
also
alter
al·tera-tion
al·tered

al·ter-ing
al·ter-nate
al·ter-nates
al·ter-nat·ing
al·ter-na-tions

al·ter-na-tive
al·ter-na-tively
al·ter-na-tives
al·ter-na-tor
al·though

al·ti-tude
al·to-gether
alu-mi-num
alum-nae
alumni

alum-nus
al·veo-lec-tomy
al·ways
am
ama-teur

ama-teurs
amaze
amazed
amaz-ing
amaz-ingly

am·bas-sa·dor
*am·bigu-ous
am·bi-tion
am·bi-tions
am·bi-tious

am·bler
am·bu-lance
am·bu-lances
amend
amenda-tory

amended
amend-ing
amend-ment
amend-ments
ami-able

*ami-ca·ble
am·mo-nia
am·mu-ni-tion
among
amongst

amor·ti-za-tion
amor·ti-za-tions
am·or-tize
am·or-tized
am·or-ti-zing

amount
amounted
amount-ing
amounts
am·phi-thea·ter

ample
am·pli-fi-ca-tion
am·pli-fied
am·pli-fier
amply

am·pu-ta·ted
amuse-ment
amuse-ments
an
an·aes-the·sia

an·aes-thetic
anal
analo-gous
*anal-ogy
analy-ses

analy-sis
ana-lyst
ana-lysts
ana-lyze
ana-lyzed

ana-lyzes
ana-lyz·ing
an·chor
an·cient
an·cil-lary

and
anent
an·es-the·sia
an·es-thetic
an·es-thet·ics

anes-the-tist
angel
angle
an·gles
an·gling

angry
an·gu-lar
ani·mal
ani-mals
ani-mated

*ani-mos·ity
ankle
an·nals
an·nealed
an·neal-ing

annex
an·nexa-tion
an·nexed
an·ni-ver-sary
an·nounce

an·nounced
an·nounce-ment
an·nounce-ments
an·nouncer
an·nounc-ing

an·noy-ance
an·noy-ing
an·nual
an·nu-ally
an·nui-ties

an·nu-ity
annul
an·nu-lar
annum
anony-mous

an·other
an·swer
an·swer-able
an·swered
an·swer-ing

an·swers
an·tago-nis·tic
an·tago-nize
an·tenna
an·thrax

an·thro-pol·ogy
an·ti-bi-ot·ics
an·tici-pate
an·tici-pated
an·tici-pates

an·tici-pat·ing
an·tici-pa-tion
an·tici-pa-tions
an·ti-dis·crimi-na-tion
an·ti-di·ver-sion

an·ti-freeze
an·ti-freezes
an·ti-pov-erty
an·ti-quated
an·tique

an·ti-trust
ant-lers
anxi-ety
anx-ious
anx-iously

any
any-body
any-body's
any-more
any·one

any-thing
any-time
any·way
any-where
apart

apart-ment
apart-ments
apa·thy
aphid
apiece

apolo-gies
apolo-gize
apol-ogy
ap·pall-ing
ap·pa-ra·tus

ap·parel
ap·par-ent
ap·par-ently
ap·peal
ap·pealed

ap·peal-ing
ap·peals
ap·pear
ap·pear-ance
ap·pear-ances

ap·peared
ap·pear-ing
ap·pears
ap·pel-lant
ap·pel-late

ap·pen-dec-tomy
ap·pended
ap·pen-dix
ap·plauded
ap·plause

apple
ap·ples
ap·pli-ance
ap·pli-ances
ap·pli-ca-bil·ity

ap·pli-ca·ble
ap·pli-cant
ap·pli-cants
ap·pli-ca-tion
ap·pli-ca-tions

ap·plied
ap·plies
apply
ap·ply-ing
ap·point

ap·pointed
ap·point-ing
ap·point-ment
ap·point-ments
ap·por-tioned

ap·por-tion·ing
ap·por-tion-ment
ap·praisal
ap·prais-als
ap·praise

ap·praised
ap·praiser
ap·prais-ers
ap·prais-ing
ap·pre-cia·ble

ap·pre-ci·ate
ap·pre-ci-ated
ap·pre-ci-ates
ap·pre-ci-at·ing
ap·pre-cia-tion

ap·pre-cia-tive
ap·pre-cia-tively
*ap·pren-tice
ap·prise
ap·prised

ap·proach
ap·proached
ap·proaches
ap·proach-ing
ap·pro-pri·ate

ap·pro-pri-ated
ap·pro-pri-ately
ap·pro-pria-tion
ap·pro-pria-tions
ap·prov-able

ap·proval
ap·prov-als
ap·prove
ap·proved
ap·prov-ing

ap·proxi-mate
ap·proxi-mated
ap·proxi-mately
ap·proxi-mat·ing
ap·proxi-ma-tion

apri-cot
aprons
apt
ap·ti-tude
ap·ti-tudes

aptly
aq·ue-ducts
ar·bi-trar·ily
ar·bi-trary
*ar·bi-tra-tion

arbor
arch
arched
arches
ar·chi-tect

ar·chi-tects
ar·chi-tec-tural
ar·chi-tec-ture
ar·chi-vist
ar·du-ous

are
area
areas
arena
aren't

argue
ar·gued
ar·gu-ing
ar·gu-ment
ar·gu-ments

ar·gyle
arise
arisen
arises
aris-ing

arith-me·tic
arm
ar·ma-ture
arm-chairs
armed

ar·mies
ar·mory
arms
army
aroma

aro-matic
arose
around
aroused
ar·range

ar·ranged
ar·range-ment
ar·range-ments
ar·ranges
ar·rang-ing

array
ar·rear
ar·rear-ages
ar·rears
ar·rested

ar·rests
ar·rival
ar·riv-als
ar·rive
ar·rived

ar·rives
ar·riv-ing
*ar·ro-gant
arrow
ar·row-head

ar·senic
*arson
art
art-craft
ar·te-rial

ar·te-ries
art-fully
*ar·thri-tis
ar·ti-cle
ar·ti-cles

ar·ti-fi-cial
art·ist
ar·tis-tic
ar·tis-ti·cally
art-tists

arts
art-work
as
as·bes-tos
as·cer-tain

as·cer-tain·ing
as·cribe
ash
ashamed
ashes

aside
*asi-nine
ask
asked
ask·ing

asks
as·pect
as·pects
aspen
as·phalt

*as·pire
as·pi-rin
as·sault
as·sem-blage
as·sem-ble

as·sem-bled
as·sem-blies
as·sem-bling
as·sem-bly
as·sem·bly-man

as·sented
as·serted
as·serts
as·sess
as·sessed

as·sess-ing
as·sess-ment
as·sess-ments
as·ses-sor
as·ses-sors

asset
as·sets
as·sign
as·signed
as·signee

as·sign-ing
as·sign-ment
as·sign-ments
*as·simi-late
as·simi-la-tion

as·sist
as·sis-tance
as·sis-tant
as·sis-tants
as·sis·tant-ship

as·sis·tant-ships
as·sisted
as·sist-ing
as·sists
as·so-ci·ate

as·so-ci·ated
as·so-ci·ates
as·so-cia-ting
as·so-cia-tion
as·so-cia-tions

as·sorted
as·sort-ment
as·sort-ments
as·sume
as·sumed

as·sumes
as·sum-ing
as·sump-tion
as·sump-tions
as·sur-ance

as·sur-ances
as·sure
as·sured
as·sureds
as·sures

as·sur-ing
as·ter-isk
as·ter-isks
asthma
asth-matic

asth-mat·ics
*as·ton-ish-ment
as·tound-ing
astray
as·trin-gents

as·tro-nom-ical
as·tute
at
ate
ath-letic

ath-leti-cally
ath-let·ics
atlas
at·mo-sphere
at·mo-spheric

atomic
atoms
at·tach
at·ta-che
at·tached

at·taches
at·tach-ing
at·tach-ment
at·tach-ments
at·tack

at·tack-ing
at·tacks
at·tain
at·tain-able
at·tained

at·tain-ing
at·tain-ment
at·tempt
at·tempted
at·tempt-ing

at·tempts
at·tend
at·ten-dance
at·ten-dant
at·ten-dants

at·tended
at·ten-dees
at·tend-ing
at·tends
at·ten-tion

*at·test
at·tested
attic
at·ti-tude
at·ti-tudes

at·tor-ney
attorney–at–law
at·tor-neys
at·tract
at·tracted

at·tract-ing
at·trac-tions
at·trac-tive
at·trac-tively
at·trac-tive-ness

at·tracts
at·trib-ut-able
*at·trib-ute
at·trib-uted
at·trib-utes

auc-tion
auc-tions
*au·di-ble
au·di-ence
au·di-ences

audio
audio–visual
audit
au·dit-ing
au·di-tion

au·di-tor
au·di-to-rium
au·di-to-ri·ums
au·di-tors
au·dits

auger
aug-ment
aug-mented
aunt
aus-pices

aus-pi-cious
au·then-tic
au·thor
au·thored
au·thori-ta-tive

au·thori-ta-tively
au·thori-ties
au·thor-ity
au·tho-ri-za-tion
au·tho-rize

au·tho-rized
au·tho-rizes
au·tho-riz·ing
au·thors
auto

au·to-claved
au·to-graph
au·to-mate
au·to-mates
au·to-matic

au·to-mati-cally
au·to-mat·ing
au·to-ma-tion
au·to-mo-bile
au·to-mo-biles

au·to-mo-tive
au·ton-omy
*au·topsy
autos
auto-trans·former

au·tumn
aux-il-ia-ries
aux-il-iary
avail
availa-bil·ity

avail-able
avail-ing
avails
ava-lanche
ave·nue

ave-nues
av·er-age
av·er-aged
av·er-ages
av·er-ag·ing

avert
averted
avia-tion
avia-tor
*avo·ca-tion

avoid
avoid-ance
avoided
avoid-ing
await

await-ing
awake
award
awarded
award-ing

awards
aware
aware-ness
away
awful

aw·fully
awk-ward
awry
ax
*axi-omatic

axle
axles
aza-leas

B

ba·bies
baby
baby's
bac·ca-lau-re·ate
bache-lor

back
back-bone
back-charge
backed
back-ground

back-grounds
back-guard
back-haul
back-hoe
back-hoes

back-ing
back-log
backs
back-scat·ter
back-side

back-slide
backup
back-ward
back-wards
back-work

bac-te·ria
bac-te-ri-cide
bad
badge
badges

badly
bad-min·ton
baf·fle
bag
bag-gage

bagged
bag-ging
bags
bait
baits

baked
baker
ba·kers
bak·ery
bal-ance

bal-anced
bal-ances
bal-an-cing
bal·co-nies
bal·cony

bald
bale
baler
bales
ball

bal-last
bal-lasts
bal·lot
bal-lot·ing
bal-lots

ball-room
balls
bal·sam
ban
ba·nana

band
ban-dage
bands
band-wagon
banged

ban·ish-ment
bank
banker
bank-ers
bank-ing

bank-rupt
bank-ruptcy
banks
ban·ner
ban-ners

ban-quet
ban-quets
bar
bar-be-cue
bar-ber

bard
bare
barely
bar-gain
bar-gain-ing

bar-gains
barge
bari-tone
bark
bark-ers

bar-ley
barn
ba-rome-ter
*bar-rage
barred

bar-rel
bar-reled
bar-rels
bar-ri-cade
bar-ring

bars
base
base-ball
base-balls
based

base-ment
base-ments
bases
basic
ba-si-cally

ba-sics
basin
bas-ing
basis
bas-ket

bas-ket-ball
bas-kets
bass
bas-set
bass-wood

batch
batches
bated
bath
bathe

bath-houses
bath-ing
bath-room
bath-rooms
baths

baton
bat-ter
bat-ter-ies
bat-tery
bat-tle

bat-tle-ground
bat-tles
bawls
bay
be

beach
beaches
bea-dle
beam
beamer

beam-ing
beams
bean
beans
bear

bearer
bear-ing
bear-ings
bears
beast

beat
beaten
beat-ing
beats
beau-ti-ful

beau-ti-fully
beau-ti-fy-ing
beauty
bea-ver
bea-vers

be-came
be-cause
beck
be-come
be-comes

be-com-ing
bed
bed-ded
bed-ding
bed-lam

bed-pan
bed-rid-den
bed-room
bed-rooms
beds

bed-sores
bed-spreads
bee
beech
beef

been
beer
bees-wax
beet
bee-tles

beets
be-fall
be-fore
beg
began

begin
be-gin-ning
be-gins
*be-grudge
begun

be-half
*be-have
be-hav-ior
be-hav-ioral
be-hind

be-hooves
beige
being
be-lated
be-lat-edly

be-lief
be-liefs
be-lieve
be-lieved
be-liever

be-lieves
be-liev-ing
bell
*bel-lig-er-ence
bells

bell-weth-ers
be-long
be-longed
be-long-ing
be-long-ings

be-longs
below
belt
belts
bench

benches
bend
bend-ing
bends
be-neath

*bene-fac-tor
bene-fi-cial
bene-fi-ci-aries
bene-fi-ci-ary
bene-fit

bene-fited
bene-fit-ing
bene-fits
*be-nevo-lence
bent

be-queathed
be-quest
be-quests
*be-reave-ment
berms

berry
berth
berths
be-seech
be-side

be-sides
be-siege
be-sieged
*be-smirch
be-speak

best
be-stow
bests
bet
*be-trothal

bets
bet-ter
bet-ter-ment
bet-ter-ments
be-tween

bevel
bev-eled
bev-er-age
bev-er-ages
be-wil-dered

be-yond
bezel
bible
bi-bles
bib-li-og-ra-phies

bib-li-og-ra-phy
*bi-cy-cle
bid
bid-der
bid-ders

bid-ding
bids
bi·en-nial
bi·en-nium
big

big·ger
big-gest
bill
bill-board
billed

bil·let
bil-lets
bill-fold
bill-folds
bill-ing

bill-ings
bil-lion
bil-lions
bills
bi·monthly

bin
bi·nary
bi·na-tional
bind
binder

bind-ers
bind-ing
bind-ings
bins
bio·chem-is·try

bio·graph-ical
bio·log-ical
bi·olo-gist
bi·ol-ogy
bi·plane

birch
bird
birds
birth
birth-day

bishop
bit
bite
bits
bit·ter

bit-ter·est
bit-terly
bit·ter-sweet
black
*black-mail

black-smith
black-strap
black-top
blad-der
blade

blades
blame
blank
blan-ket
blan-kets

blanks
blas-phemy
blast
blasted
blast-ing

bled
bleed
bleed-ing
bleeds
blem-ish

blem-ishes
blend
blended
blender
blend-ing

blends
bless
blessed
bless-ing
bless-ings

blew
blind
blinds
*bliss-ful
blitz

block
blocked
blocker
block-ing
blocks

blond
blood
bloom
bloom-ing
blooms

blot-ter
blot-ters
blouses
blow
blower

blow-ers
blow-ing
blown
blow-out
blows

blue
blue-gill
blue-green
blue-print
blue-prints

blues
bluff
bluffs
*blun-der
blun-ders

*bluntly
blur
board
boards
boast

boat
boat-ing
boats
bob
bob·bin

bob-white
bod·ies
bod·ily
body
boggy

boil
boiled
boiler
boil-ers
boil-ing

*bois-ter·ous
bold
bo·lero
*bol-ster
bolt

bolts
bom-bard·ing
bomb-ing
bombs
bona fide

*bo·nanza
bond
bonded
bond-hold·ers
bond-ing

bonds
*bonds-man
bone
bones
bonus

bo·nuses
book
book-cases
book-deal·ers
booked

book-ing
book-ings
book-keeper
book-keep·ers
book-keep·ing

book-let
book-lets
book-plate
book-plates
books

book-seller
book-store
boom
*boom-er·ang
boon

boost
booster
boost-ing
booth
booths

boots
bor·der
bor-de-reau
bor-der·ing
bor·der-line

bor-ders
bore
*bor·ing
born
borne

bor·row
bor-rowed
bor-rower
bor-row·ers
bor-row·ing

bor-rows
boss
bosses
bot·any
both

bother
both-ered
both-er·ing
bot·tle
bot·tle-necks

bot-tlers
bot-tles
bot·tom
bot·tom-lands
bot-toms

bough
bought
boul-der
bou·le-vard
bounce

bound
bounda-ries
bound-ary
bounded
boun-ti·ful

bou-quets
bour-bon
bout
bouts
bow

bow·els
bowl
bowl-ing
bowls
box

boxed
boxer
boxes
box·ing
boy

boy-cott
boy-hood
boys
brace
braced

brac-ing
bracket
brack-ets
brack-ish
brag-garts

braid
brains
brake
brakes
branch

branches
brand
branded
brand-ing
brands

brass
bras-sieres
brat
brav-ery
breach

bread
breadth
break
break-age
break-away

break-down
break-downs
breaker
break-ers
break-fast

break-fasts
break-ing
breaks
breath
breathe

breath-ing
breath-tak·ing
bred
breeder
breed-ers

breed-ing
breeds
breezy
breth-ren
brev-ity

brewer
brew-er·ies
brew-ery
brick
brick-bats

bricks
brick—veneered
*bride-groom
bridge
bridges

brief
briefed
brief-est
brief-ing
briefly

briefs
bri-gade
bri-gades
bright
brighten

brighter
bril-liance
bril-liant
bril-liantly
bring

bring-ing
brings
brisk
broached
broad

broad-cast
broad-cast-ers
broad-cast-ing
broad-casts
broaden

broad-ened
broad-en-ing
broader
broad-est
broad-looms

broadly
broad-side
broad-sides
broad-way
bro-chure

bro-chures
brock
*brogue
broil-ers
broke

bro·ken
bro·ker
bro·ker·age
bro·kers
*bron-chial

bronze
brooch
brood
brood-ers
brook

broom
brooms
broom-stick
brother
broth·er-hood

broth-ers
brought
brown
browned
bruises

brush
brushes
bub-bled
bub-bles
buck

bucket
buck-ets
buck-ing
buckle
buck-ram

bud
bud-dies
bud·get
bud-get·ary
bud-geted

bud-get·ing
bud-gets
buds
buff
buf-falo

buffer
buff-ers
bug-gies
buggy
bugs

build
builder
build-ers
build-ing
build-ings

builds
buildup
built
built–in
built–up

bulb
bulbs
bulge
bulg-ing
bulk

bulky
bull
bull-dozer
bul·let
bul-le·tin

bul-le·tins
bul-lock
bulls
bumper
bump-ers

bump-ing
bumps
bun·dle
bun-dles
bunk

*buoy-ancy
bur·den
bur-dened
bur-dens
bur·den-some

bu·reau
bu·reau-cracy
bu·reau-crats
bu·reaus
bur-glar

bur·glar-proof
bur-glary
bur·ial
bur·ied
bur-lapped

bur-laps
burn
burned
burner
burn-ing

burns
bur·si-tis
burst-ing
bus
buses

bush
bush-els
bushes
bush-ing
bush-ings

bus·ier
busi-est
busi-ness
busi-nesses
busi·ness-man

busi·ness-men
bust
busy
but
bu·tane

but·ler
but·ter
but·ter-milk
but·ton
but·ton-holder

but-tons
butts
buy
buyer
buy·ers

buy·ing
buys
by
bylaw
by·laws

by·pass
by·pass-ing
by-product
*by·stander

C
---

cab
cab-bage
cabi-net
cabi-nets
cab·ins

cable
ca·bles
ca·ble-vi·sion
ca·chet
cadet

cafe-te·ria
cafe-te·rias
cais-son
cake
cakes

ca·lam-ity
cal-cium
cal·cu-late
cal·cu-lated
cal·cu-lat·ing

cal·cu-la-tion
cal·cu-la-tions
cal·cu-la·tor
cal·cu-la-tors
cal-culi

cal-cu·lus
cal-en·dar
cal-en·dars
calf
cali-ber

cali-bra-tion
cali-bre
calk
call
called

call-ers
call-ing
calls
*calmly
*calo-ries

cam
cam-bric
came
ca·mel-lias
cam·era

cam·era-men
cam-eras
*cam·ou-flage
camp
cam-paign

cam-paign-ing
cam-paigns
camp-ers
camp-ing
camps

cam-pus
cam-puses
can
canal
ca-nals

can-cel
can-celed
can-cel-ing
can-cel-la-tion
can-cel-la-tions

can-cels
can-cer
can-de-la-bras
can-di-dacy
can-di-date

can-di-dates
can-didly
can-dles
candy
cane

can-ker-worm
can-ker-worms
canned
can-ning
can-non

can-not
canoe
ca-noes
canon
cans

can't
*can-ta-loupe
can-teen
can-ton
can-vas

can-vass
can-yon
cap
ca-pa-bili-ties
ca-pa-bil-ity

ca-pa-ble
ca-pa-bly
ca-paci-ties
ca-paci-tors
ca-pac-ity

cap-il-lary
capi-tal
*capi-tal-ist
capi-tali-za-tion
capi-tal-ize

capi-tal-izes
capi-tol
caps
cap-tain
cap-tion

cap-tioned
cap-tion-ing
cap-ture
cap-tures
cap-tur-ing

car
carat
car-bide
car-bon
car-bon-ized

car-boni-zing
car-bons
car-boys
car-cass
car-casses

card
card-board
car-diac
car-di-nal
cards

care
cared
ca-reer
ca-reers
care-free

care-ful
care-fully
care-less
care-less-ness
cares

cargo
car-goes
car-load
car-loads
car-mine

car-ni-val
car-pen-ter
car-pen-ters
car-pen-try
car-pet

car-peted
car-pet-ing
car-pets
car-ports
car-riage

C

car-ried
car-rier
car-ri·ers
car-ries
car·rot

carry
car-ry·ing
carry–overs
cars
cart

cart-age
car·to-graph-ical
car·ton
car-tons
car-toon

car-toons
car-tridge
car-tridges
carts
cas-cade

case
case-hard·ened
cases
cash
cashed

cash-ier
cash-iers
cash-ing
cas·ing
cask

cast
cast-ers
cast-ing
cas·tle
cast-offs

casts
ca·sual
ca·su-ally
ca·su-al-ties
ca·su-alty

cat
cata-log
cata-logs
cata-loged
cata-lyst

cata-lytic
ca·tas-tro·phe
ca·tas-tro·phes
catch
catch-all

catches
catch-ing
catch–up
catchy
cate-gori-cally

cate-go·ries
cate-gory
cat·er-pil·lar
cat·er-pil-lars
cat-fish

cat·tle
cat·tle-men
cat·tle-men's
caught
*cau·li-flower

caulk-ing
cause
caused
causes
caus-ing

cau-tion
cau-tioned
cau-tiously
cav-erns
cav·iar

cay
cease
ceased
ceases
cedar

cede
ceiled
ceil-ing
ceil-ings
cele-brate

cele-brated
cele-brat·ing
cele·bra-tion
ce·leb-rity
cell

cel·lar
cel-lars
cel·lo-phane
cel·lu-lose
ce·ment

cen·sor-ship
*cen-sure
cen·sus
cent
cen·ten-nial

cen·ter
cen-tered
cen-ter·ing
cen-ters
*cen·ti-grade

*cen·ti·meter
cen·tral
*cen·trali·za·tion
cen·tral·ized
cen·trifu·gal

cen·trifu·gally
cents
cen·tum
cen·tu·ries
cen·tury

ce·ramic
ce·ram·ics
cere·mo·ni·ally
cere·mo·nies
cere·mony

cer·tain
cer·tainly
cer·tainty
cer·tifi·cate
cer·tifi·cated

cer·tifi·cates
cer·ti·fi·ca·tion
cer·ti·fi·ca·tions
cer·ti·fied
cer·ti·fies

cer·tify
cer·ti·fy·ing
chafe
chaff
chain

chains
chair
chaired
chair–lift
chair·man

chair·men
chairs
chal·lenge
chal·lenged
chal·lenges

chal·leng·ing
cham·ber
cham·bers
cham·bray
cham·ois

cham·pagne
cham·pi·ons
chance
chances
change

*change·able
changed
change·over
changes
chang·ing

chan·nel
chan·neled
chan·nels
chaos
*cha·otic

chap
chapel
chap·els
chap·ter
chap·ters

char·ac·ter
char·ac·ter·is·tic
char·ac·ter·is·tics
char·ac·teri·za·tion
char·ac·ter·ize

char·ac·ter·ized
char·ac·ters
*char·coal
charge
charge·able

charge–back
charged
charges
charg·ing
chari·ta·ble

chari·ties
char·ity
charm·ing
chart
char·ter

char·tered
charts
chase
chas·sis
*chas·tise·ment

chat
chats
chat·tel
chat·ter
chauf·feurs

cheap
cheaper
cheap·est
cheaply
check

check·book
checked
checker
check·ers
check·ing

check-list
check-lists
checks
checkup
cheer

cheer-ful
cheer-fully
cheer-ing
cheese
chem-ical

chem-icals
chem-ist
chem-is-try
chem-ists
cheques

cher-ish
cher-ished
cher-ries
cherry
chess

chest
chest-nut
chests
chews
chic

chick
chicken
chick-ens
chicks
chided

chief
chiefly
child
child-birth
child-hood

child-less
chil-dren
chil-dren's
child's
chili

chilled
china
chip
chip-board
chi-ro-prac-tic

chi-ro-prac-tor
chisel
chis-el-ing
*chiv-alry
chlo-ri-nated

chlo-ro-phyll
choco-late
choice
choices
choir

choked
chokes
choose
choos-ing
chore

chores
cho-rus
chose
cho-sen
chrome

chronic
chro-no-log-ical
chunk
chunks
church

churches
churned
churn-ing
chutes
ciga-rette

ciga-rettes
cinch
cir-cle
cir-cled
cir-cles

cir-cuit
cir-cuits
cir-cu-lar
cir-cu-lar-ize
cir-cu-lar-ized

cir-cu-lari-zing
cir-cu-lars
cir-cu-late
cir-cu-lated
cir-cu-lat-ing

cir-cu-la-tion
cir-cu-la-tors
cir-cum-stance
cir-cum-stances
cir-cum-vent

ci-ta-tion
ci-ta-tions
cite
cited
cit-ies

citi-zen
citi-zens
citi-zen-ship
cit-rus
city

civic
civil
ci·vil·ian
ci·vil·ians
civi·li·za·tion

clad
claim
claim·able
claim·ant
claim·ants

claimed
claim·ing
claims
clam·or·ing
clamps

clam·shells
clari·fi·ca·tion
clari·fied
clari·fier
clari·fies

clar·ify
clari·fy·ing
clar·ity
class
classed

classes
clas·sic
clas·sics
clas·si·fi·ca·tion
clas·si·fi·ca·tions

clas·si·fied
clas·sify
clas·si·fying
class·mates
class·room

class·rooms
class·work
clause
clauses
clay

clays
clean
cleaned
cleaner
clean·ers

clean·est
clean·ing
clean·li·ness
cleans
cleanup

clear
clear·ance
clear–cut
cleared
clearer

clear·ing
clear·ing·house
clearly
clears
cleaver

clem·ent
clergy
cler·ical
clerk
clerks

cli·ent
cli·en·tele
cli·ents
cliffs
cli·mate

cli·max
climb
climb·ing
clinic
clin·ical

cli·ni·cian
clin·ics
clip
clipped
clip·pers

clip·ping
clip·pings
clips
clock
clock·wise

clock·work
close
closed
closely
close·ness

close·out
closer
closes
clos·est
closet

clos·ets
clos·ing
clos·ings
clo·sures
cloth

clothe
clothes
cloth·ing
cloths
cloud

*cloud-burst
clouded
clouds
club
clubs

clue
*clumsy
clus-ter
clutch
clutches

clut-tered
coach
coaches
coach-ing
co-ad-just-ers

co-agu-la-tion
coal
coals
coarse
coast

coastal
coast-ers
coast-ing
coat
coated

coat-ing
coat-ings
coats
cob
cobs

cock-tail
cock-tails
cod
cod-dling
code

coded
codes
cod-ing
co-ef-fi-cient
co-ef-fi-cients

*co-erce
cof-fee
cogi-ta-tion
cog-ni-zant
*co-her-ence

coil
coils
coin
co-in-cide
co-in-ci-dence

co-in-ci-dent
coins
co-in-sur-ance
cold
colder

cole
*col-labo-rate
col-labo-ra-tion
col-lapse
*col-laps-ible

col-laps-ing
col-lar
col-lards
col-lat-eral
col-la-ting

col-la-tor
col-la-tors
col-league
col-leagues
col-lect

col-lected
col-lecti-bil-ity
col-lect-ing
col-lec-tion
col-lec-tions

col-lec-tive
col-lec-tively
col-lec-tor
col-lec-tors
col-lects

col-lege
col-leges
col-le-giate
col-li-sion
col-li-sions

col-lo-quy
col-lu-sion
co-logne
colo-nel
co-lo-nial

co-lonic
colo-nies
colony
color
col-ored

col-or-ful
col-or-ing
col-or-ists
col-ors
*co-los-sal

co-los-tomy
col-umn
co-lum-nar
col-um-nist
col-um-nists

col-umns
com·bat
com-bat·ing
combed
com·bi-na-tion

com·bi-na-tions
com-bine
com-bined
com-bines
com-bin·ing

combs
com·bus-tion
come
co·me-dian
come–on

comes
com-fort
com·fort-able
com·fort-ably
com·fort·ers

com-forts
comic
com·ing
com-mand
com-man-dant

com-mander
com-mand·ing
com·mand-ments
com-mands
com-memo-rat·ing

com-mence
com-menced
com·mence-ment
com-mences
com-menc·ing

com-mend
com-mend-able
com·men-da-tion
com·men-da-tions
com·men-da-tory

com-mended
com-mend·ing
com·men-su-rate
com-ment
com-men-tary

com·men-ta·tor
com·men-ta·tors
com-mented
com-ment·ing
com-ments

com-merce
com·mer-cial
com·mer-cially
com·mer-cials
com·mis-sion

com·mis-sioned
com·mis-sioner
com·mis-sion·ers
com·mis-sion·ing
com·mis-sions

com·mit
com·mit-ment
com·mit-ments
com-mit·ted
com-mit·tee

com·mit·tee-men
com·mit-tees
com·mit-ting
com-mode
com·modi-ties

com-mod·ity
com-mo-dore
com-mon
com-mon·est
com-monly

com-mon-place
com-mon-wealth
com-mon-wealths
com-mo-tion
com-mu-ni-cate

com-mu-ni-ca·ting
com-mu-ni-ca-tion
com-mu-ni-ca-tions
com-mu-ni-ca-tive
com-mu-nism

com-mu-nist
com-mu-ni-ties
com-mu-nity
com-mute
com-pact

com-pactly
com·pa-nies
com-pan·ion
com-pany
com·pa-ra-bil·ity

com·pa-ra-ble
com-para-tive
com-para-tively
com-pare
com-pared

com-pares
com-par·ing
com-pari·son
com-pari-sons
com·part-ment

com·part-ments
com-pat-ible
*com·pel
com-pelled
com-pel-ling

com·pen-sa·ble
com·pen-sate
com·pen-sated
com·pen-sa-ting
com·pen-sa-tion

com-pete
com·pe-tence
com·pe-tent
com·pe-tently
com-pet·ing

com·pe-ti-tion
com·peti-tive
com·peti-tively
com·peti·tor
com-peti-tors

com·pi-la-tion
com-pile
com-piled
com-pil·ing
*com·pla-cent

com-plain
com-plained
com-plain·ing
com-plains
com-plaint

com-plaints
com·ple-ment
com-plete
com-pleted
com-pletely

com·plete-ness
com-plet·ing
com·ple-tion
com-plex
com-plex·ion

com·plexi-ties
com·plex·ity
com·pli-ance
com·pli-cated
com·pli-cates

com·pli-ca-tion
com-plied
com·pli-ment
com·pli-men-tary
com·pli-mented

com·pli-ment·ing
com·pli-ments
com·ply
com·ply·ing
com·po-nent

com·po-nents
com-pose
com-posed
com-poser
com-pos·ite

com·po-si-tion
com-pound
com-pounded
com-pound·ing
com-pounds

com·pre-hen-sion
com·pre-hen-sive
com·pre-hen-sively
com·pres-sion
com·pres-sioned

com-pres·sor
com-pres-sors
com-prise
com-prised
com-prises

com-pris·ing
com·pro-mise
comp-trol·ler
com-pul-sion
com-pul-sory

com-pu-ta-tion
com-pu-ta-tions
com-pute
com-puted
com-puter

com-put-er-ized
com-put·ers
com-put·ing
com-rade
con-ceal

con-cealed
*con-cede
con·ceiv-able
con·ceiv-ably
con-ceived

con·cen-trate
con·cen-tra·ted
con·cen-tra-ting
con·cen-tra-tion
con·cen-tra-tions

con-cept
con·cep-tion
con-cepts
con-cern
con-cerned

con-cern·ing
con-cerns
con-cert
con-certed
con-certs

con·ces-sion
con·ces-sional
con·ces-sions
con-cise
con-cisely

con-clave
con-claves
con-clude
con-cluded
con-cludes

con-clud·ing
con·clu-sion
con·clu-sions
con·clu-sive
con·clu-sively

con-crete
con-cur
con-curred
con-cur-rence
con-cur-rently

con-cur-ring
con·dem-na·tion
con-demned
con-demn·ing
con·den-sate

con-densed
con-den·ser
con·di-tion
con·di-tional
con·di-tioned

con·di-tioner
con·di-tion·ing
con·di-tions
con·do-lences
con·du-cive

con-duct
con-ducted
con-duct·ing
con-duct·ive
con-duc·tor

con-duc·tors
con-ducts
con-duit
cone
cones

con·fer
con·fer-ence
con·fer-ences
con-ferred
con·fer-ring

con-fess
*con·fes-sion
con·fes-sions
*con-fide
con·fi-dence

con·fi-dent
con·fi-den-tial
con·fi-den-ti-al·ity
con·fi-den-tially
con·fi-dently

con-figu-ra-tion
con-fine
con-fined
con-fine-ment
con-fines

con-fin·ing
con-firm
con·fir-ma-tion
con·fir-ma-tions
con·fir-ma-tory

con-firmed
con-firm·ing
con-firms
con·fis-ca-tory
con-flict

con-flict·ing
con-flicts
con·flu-ence
con-form
con-formed

con-form·ing
*con-form·ity
con-forms
con-front
con-fronted

con-front·ing
con-fuse
con-fused
con-fus·ing
con·fu-sion

*con-gen·ial
con-gested
con·ges-tion
con·gratu-late
con·gratu-lated

con·gratu-la-tion
con·gratu-la-tions
con·gratu-la-tory
con·gre-gate
con·gre-gated

con·gre- ga-tion
con·gre- ga-tions
con·gress
con·gresses
con·gres-sio·nal

con·gress-man
con·gress-men
con·jec-tural
con·junc-tion
con-nect

con-nected
con-nect·ing
con·nec-tion
con·nec-tions
*con-note

con-quer·ing
con-quest
con-science
con·sci-en-tious
con·sci-en-tiously

con-scious
*con·se-cra-tion
con·secu-tive
*con- sen·sus
con-sent

con-sented
con·se-quence
con·se-quences
con·se-quent
con·se-quently

con·ser-va-tion
con·serva-tism
con·serva-tive
con·serva-tively
con·serva-tors

con-serva-tory
con-serve
con-serv·ing
con-sider
con-sid-er-able

con·sid-er-ably
con·sid-era-tion
con·sid-era-tions
con·sid-ered
con·sid-er·ing

con·sid-ers
con-sign
con-signed
con-signee
con-sign·ees

con-sign·ing
con·sign-ment
con-sist
con-sisted
con·sis-tent

con-sis-tently
con-sist·ing
con-sists
con-sole
con-soles

con·soli-date
con·soli-dated
con·soli-dat·ing
con·soli-da-tion
con·so-nance

con·sor-tium
con-spicu·ous
con-spire
con-spired
con-stant

con-stantly
con·stel-la-tion
con-stitu·ent
con-stitu-ents
con·sti-tute

con·sti-tuted
con·sti-tutes
con·sti-tu-tion
con·sti-tu-tional
con-struct

con-structed
con-struct·ing
con·struc-tion
con·struc-tions
con·struc-tive

con·struc-tively
con- struc-tor
con-strued
con·sul
con-sult

con-sul-tant
con-sul-tants
con·sul-ta-tion
con·sul-ta-tions
con·sul-ta-tive

con-sulted
con-sult·ing
con-sume
con-sumed
con-sumer

con-sum·ers
con-sum·ing
con-sum-mate
con-sum-mated
con·sump-tion

con-tact
con-tacted
con-tact-ing
con-tacts
con-tain

con-tained
con-tainer
con-tain-ers
con-tain-ing
con-tains

con-tami-na-tion
con-tem-plate
con-tem-plated
con-tem-plates
con-tem-plat-ing

con-tem-pla-tive
con-tem-po-rar-ies
*con-tem-po-rary
*con-tempt-ible
con-tend

con-tent
con-ten-tion
con-tents
con-test
con-test-able

con-tes-tant
con-tested
con-tests
con-text
con-tigu-ous

con-ti-nence
con-ti-nen-tal
con-tin-gen-cies
con-tin-gency
con-tin-gent

con-tinu-able
con-tinual
con-tinu-ally
con-tinu-ance
con-tinu-ation

con-tinue
con-tin-ued
con-tin-ues
con-tinu-ing
con-ti-nu-ity

con-tinu-ous
con-tinu-ously
con-tour
con-tours
con-tract

con-tracted
con-tract-ing
con-trac-tor
con-trac-tors
con-tracts

con-trac-tual
con-tra-dict
con-tra-dicted
con-trary
con-trast

con-trasted
con-tra-ven-tion
con-trib-ute
con-trib-uted
con-trib-utes

con-trib-ut-ing
con-tri-bu-tion
con-tri-bu-tions
con-tribu-tor
con-tribu-tors

con-tribu-tory
*con-trive
con-trol
con-trol-la-ble
con-trolled

con-trol-ler
con-trol-lers
con-trol-ling
con-trols
con-tro-ver-sial

con-tro-versy
con-tu-sions
con-va-les-cent
con-ve-nience
con-ve-niences

con-ve-nient
con-ve-niently
con-ven-ing
con-ven-tion
con-ven-tional

con-ven-tions
con-ver-sant
con-ver-sa-tion
con-ver-sa-tions
con-versely

con-ver-sion
con-ver-sions
con-vert
con-verted
con-verter

con-vert-ers
con-verti-bil-ity
con-vert-ible
con-vert-ibles
con-vert-ing

con·verts
con·vex
con·vex·ity
con·vey
con·vey-ance

con·vey-ances
con·veyed
con·vey·ing
con·veyor
con·vic·tion

con·vic-tions
con·vince
con·vinced
con·vinces
con·vinc·ing

con·vinc-ingly
con·vo-ca-tion
*con·voy
cook
cooked

cook-ies
cook-ing
cool
cooled
cooler

cool-ing
coon
co–op
coop
co·op-er·ate

co·op-er-ated
co·op-era-ting
co·op-era-tion
co·op-era-tive
co·op-era-tively

co·op-era-tives
co·op-era-tor
co–ops
co·or-di-nate
co·or-di-nated

co·or-di-na-ting
co·or-di-na-tion
co·or-di-na·tor
co·or-di-na-tors
co–owner

co–owners
cope
cop·ied
cop·ier
cop-iers

cop·ies
cop·per
copy
copy-ing
copy-read·ers

copy-right
cord
cor-dial
cor-dial·ity
cor-dially

cords
cor-du·roy
core
corn
cor·ner

cor-ners
cor·net
co·rona
*cor-po·ral
cor·po-rate

cor·po-ra-tion
cor·po-ra-tions
corps
*corpse
cor·pus

cor·ral
cor-rect
cor-rected
cor-rect·ing
cor·rec-tion

cor·rec-tional
cor·rec-tions
cor·rec-tive
cor-rectly
cor·rect-ness

cor·re-late
cor·re-lated
cor·re-lates
cor·re-la-ting
cor·re-la-tion

cor·re-la-tions
cor·re-spond
cor·re-sponded
cor·re-spon-dence
cor·re-spon-dent

cor·re-spon-dents
cor·re-spond·ing
cor·re-spond-ingly
*cor·ri-dor
cor·robo-rate

cor·robo-rated
cor-rod·ing
cor-ro-sion
cor·ru-gated
*cor-rupt

cor-sage
co·se-cant
co·sign-ers
cos-metic
cos-met·ics

cos·mos
co·spon-sor
co·spon-sor-ship
cost
costa

cost-ing
cost-ings
costly
costs
cos-tume

cos-tumes
cot
cot-tage
cot-tages
cot·ton

cot-tons
cot·ton-tail
couch
cou-gars
could

couldn't
coun-cil
coun·cil-men
coun-cils
coun-sel

coun-sel·ing
coun-selor
coun-sel·ors
coun-sels
count

counted
coun-ter
*coun·ter-act
coun·ter-bal·ance
coun·ter-bal·anced

coun·ter-feit
coun·ter-part
coun·ter-parts
coun-ters
coun·ter-sign

coun·ter-sig·na·ture
coun·ter-signed
coun-ties
count-ing
count-less

coun-tries
coun-try
counts
county
coupe

cou·ple
cou-pled
cou-plers
cou-ples
cou-plings

cou·pon
cou-pons
cour-age
*cou·ra-geous
cou-rier

course
courses
court
cour-te·ous
cour·te-ously

cour·te-sies
cour-tesy
court-house
court-ing
court-room

courts
cove
cove-nant
cove-nants
cover

cov-er·age
cov·er-ages
cov·er-alls
cov-ered
cov-er·ing

cov-er-ings
cov·ers
co·verted
co·vert-ing
cow

cow·ard
*cow·ard·ice
cow·boy
cowl
co−worker

co−workers
cow-poke
cows
crack
crack-down

crack-ing
cra·dle
craft
crafts
crafts-man

crammed
cramped
crane
crank-case
crashes

crated
crat-ing
crav-ing
crawls
crayon

cray-ons
cream
creamy
cre·ate
cre-ated

cre-ates
cre-at·ing
crea-tion
crea-tions
crea-tive

crea-tiv·ity
crea-ture
cre·den-tial
cre·den-tials
cre-denza

credi-bil·ity
credit
cred·it-able
cred-ited
cred-it·ing

credi-tor
credi-tors
cred-its
creed
creeds

creek
creep
creep-ing
creeps
creo-sote

creo-soted
crept
crest
crew
crews

cried
cries
crime
crimes
crimi-nal

crimi-nals
crim-son
crip-ple
crip-pled
crip-pling

cri·sis
crisp
cri-te·ria
cri-te-rion
critic

crit-ical
criti-cally
criti-cism
criti-cisms
criti-cize

criti-cized
crit-ics
crock-ery
crook
crooked

crop
crops
cross
crossed
crosses

cross-ing
cross-ings
cross=section
cross-wise
cro·ton

crow
crowd
crowded
crown
cru-cial

crude
cruel
cruise
cruises
cru-sade

cru-sader
crush
crushed
crush-ing
crutches

crux
cry·ing
crys-tal
*crys·tal-lize
crys·tal-liz·ing

crys-tals
cub·age
cube
cubic
cu·cum-ber

cuff
cull
culled
cull-ing
cul·mi-nate

cul·mi-nates
cul·mi-na-tion
cul·ti-vate
cul·ti-vated
cul·ti-va-tion

cul-tural
cul-tur-ally
cul-tures
cul·ver
cul-vert

cu·mu-la-tive
*cun-ningly
cup
cup-board
cur-able

curb
curbed
curb-ing
curbs
cure

cured
cures
cur·few
cur·ing
cu·ri-os·ity

cu·ri-ous
curl-ers
cur·ren-cies
cur-rency
cur-rent

cur-rently
cur-rents
cur-ric·ula
cur-ricu·lar
cur-ricu·lum

cur-sory
cur-tail
cur-tailed
cur·tail-ment
cur-tain

cur-tains
curve
curved
curves
cush-ion

cush-ioned
cush-ion·ing
cush-ions
cuss
cus-tard

cus·to-dial
cus·to-dian
cus-tody
cus-tom
cus·tom-ar·ily

cus-tom·ary
cus-tomer
cus-tom·ers
cus-toms
cut

cut-back
cut-backs
cut·off
cut·out
cut-over

cuts
cut·ters
cut-ting
cut-worms
cycle

cy·cles
cy·clones
cyl-in·der
cyl·in-ders

D

dad
dads
dai-lies
daily
dair-ies

dairy
dairy-man
dam
dam·age
dam-aged

dam-ages
dam-ag·ing
dam·ask
damp
damp-ened

damp-ness
dams
dam-site
dance
danc-ers

dances	dealer	de·ce-dents
danc-ing	deal-ers	*de·ceive
dan·ger	deal·er-ship	de·cel-er·ate
dan-ger·ous	deal·er-ships	de·cel-era-tion
dan·ger-ously	deal-ing	de·cent
dan-gers	deal-ings	*de·cep-tive
dan-gling	deals	de·cide
dar·ing	dealt	de·cided
dark	dean	de·cides
darker	dean-ery	de·cid-ing
dark-ness	deans	deci-mal
dar-ling	dear	de·ci-sion
darn	dearly	de·ci-sions
darts	death	de·ci-sive
dash	death-less	deck
data	deaths	decks
date	*de·bat-able	dec·la-ra-tion
dated	de·bate	dec·la-ra-tions
dates	de·bated	de·clare
dat·ing	de·ben-ture	de·clared
daugh-ter	de·ben-tures	de·clares
daugh-ters	debit	de·cline
dav·en-port	deb·its	de·clined
day	de·bris	de·clines
day-light	debt	de·clin-ing
day-lights	debtor	de·con-trol
days	debt-ors	de·con-trolled
day-time	debts	deco-rate
dea-cons	de·cade	deco-rated
dead	de·cades	deco-rat·ing
dead-beat	decal	deco-ra·tion
dead-line	de·cals	deco-ra-tions
dead-lines	decay	deco-ra·tive
deaf	de·ceased	deco-ra·tor
deal	de·ce-dent	deco-ra·tors

de·crease
de·creased
de·creases
de·creas-ing
de·cree

dedi-cate
dedi-cated
dedi-cat·ing
dedi-ca·tion
dedi-ca·tions

de·duct
de·ducted
de·ducti-bil·ity
de·duct-ible
de·duct-ibles

de·duct-ing
de·duc-tion
de·duc-tions
deed
deeded

deeds
deem
deemed
deep
deeper

deep-est
deeply
deer
de·face
de·fac-ing

de·fat-ted
de·fault
de·faulted
de·fault-ing
de·faults

de·feat
de·feated
de·feats
de·fect
de·fec-tive

de·fects
de·fend
de·fen-dant
de·fen-dants
de·fended

de·fend-ers
de·fend-ing
de·fense
de·fenses
*de·fen-si·ble

defer
de·fer-ment
de·fer-ral
de·ferred
de·fi-cien-cies

de·fi-ciency
*de·fi-cient
defi-cit
defi-cits
de·fine

de·fined
de·fin-ing
defi-nite
defi-nitely
defi-ni·tion

defi-ni·tions
de·fini-tively
de·flec-tions
de·fo·li-ants
de·fo·li-ated

de·formed
de·fraud-ing
de·fray
de·froster
*de·funct

*de·gen-era-tion
*deg·ra-da-tion
de·gree
de·grees
de·hy-drated

de·hy-drat·ing
delay
de·layed
de·lay-ing
de·lays

dele-gate
dele-gated
dele-gates
dele·ga-tion
de·lete

de·leted
de·let-ing
de·le-tions
de·lib-er·ate
de·lib·er-ately

de·lib-era-ting
de·lib-era-tions
deli-cate
de·li-cious
de·lighted

de·light-ful
de·light-fully
de·line-ated
de·lin-quen-cies
de·lin-quency

de·lin-quent
de·liver
de·liv-er·able
de·liv-ered
de·liv-er·ies

de·liv-er·ing
de·liv-ers
de·liv-ery
delta
de·luded

del·uge
del-uged
de·luxe
delve
delv-ing

de·mand
de·manded
de·mand-ing
de·mands
de·moc-racy

demo-cratic
demo-crats
de·mol-ished
de·mol-ish·ing
de·mo-li-tion

dem·on-strat-able
dem·on-strate
dem·on-strated
dem·on-strates
dem·on-strat·ing

dem·on-stra-tion
dem·on-stra·tions
dem·on-stra·tor
dem·on-stra-tors
*de·mor-al·ize

de·mount-able
de·mur-rage
de·na-tured
de·nial
de·nied

de·nier
denim
den·ims
de·nomi-nated
de·nomi-na-tion

de·nomi-na-tional
de·nomi-na-tions
de·nomi-na·tor
de·notes
de·not-ing

*de·nounce
dense
den·si-fied
den-sity
dent

den·tal
dented
den·ti-frice
den-tist
den-tistry

den-tists
dents
deny
de·ny-ing
*de·odor-ant

de·odor-izer
de·part
de·part-ment
de·part-men·tal
de·part-ments

de·par-ture
de·pend
de·penda-bil·ity
de·pend-able
de·pended

de·pen-dence
de·pen-dency
de·pen-dent
de·pen-dents
de·pend-ing

de·pends
de·pict
de·pict-ing
de·picts
de·plete

de·pleted
de·ple-tion
de·plores
de·posit
de·pos-ited

de·pos-it·ing
depo·si-tion
depo·si-tions
de·posi-tor
de·posi-to·ries

de·posi-tors
de·posi-tory
de·pos-its
depot
de·pre-cia·ble

de·pre-ci·ate
de·pre-ci·ated
de·pre-cia-tion
de·pressed
de·press-ing

de·pres-sion
de·pri-va-tion
de·prive
de·prived
depth

depths
dep·uty
de·rive
de·rived
de·rives

der·ma-to-logic
de·roga-tory
*de·scend-ant
de·scend-ing
de·scent

de·scribe
de·scribed
de·scribes
de·scrib-ing
de·scrip-tion

de·scrip-tions
de·scrip-tive
des·ert
de·serted
de·serve

de·served
de·serves
de·serv-ing
de·sign
des·ig-nate

des·ig-nated
des·ig-nates
des·ig-nat·ing
des·ig-na-tion
des·ig-na-tions

de·signed
de·signer
de·sign-ers
de·sign-ing
de·signs

de·sira-bil·ity
de·sir-able
de·sire
de·sired
de·sires

de·sir-ing
de·sir-ous
de·sist
desk
desks

de·spair
des·per-ately
de·spite
des·ti-na-tion
des·ti-na-tions

des-tined
des·ti-tute
de·stroy
de·stroyed
de·stroy-ers

de·stroy-ing
de·stroys
de·struc-tion
de·struc-tive
de·tach

de·tach-able
de·tach-ing
de·tail
de·tailed
de·tail-ing

de·tails
*de·tain
de·tect
de·tected
de·tect-ing

de·tec-tion
de·ten-tion
deter
de·ter-gent
de·ter-gents

*de·te-rio-rate
de·te-rio-ra-tion
de·ter-mi-na-tion
de·ter-mine
de·ter-mined

de·ter-mines
de·ter-min-ing
de·terred
de·ter-rent
de·tracted

det·ri-ment
det·ri-men-tal
de·valu-ation
dev·as-tated
dev·as-tat·ing

de·velop
de·vel-oped
de·vel-oper
de·vel-op·ers
de·vel-op·ing

de·vel-op-ment
de·vel-op-men·tal
de·vel-op-ments
de·vel-ops
de·vi-ate

de·via-tion
de·via-tions
de·vice
de·vices
dev-il·ish

de·vi-ous
de·vise
de·vised
de·vi-see
de·vises

de·vote
de·voted
de·vot-ing
de·vo-tion
de·vour

dex-trose
dia-be·tes
*dia-betic
*di·ag-nose
di·ag-no·ses

di·ag-no·sis
di·ag-nos·tic
di·ago-nal
dia-gram
dia·gram-matic

dia-grams
dials
di·aly-sis
di·ame-ter
di·ame-ters

dia-mond
dia-monds
dia·per
*dia-phragm
dice

dic-tate
dic-tated
dic-tates
dic-tat·ing
dic·ta-tion

dic·ta-tional
dic-tion·ary
did
didn't
die

died
dies
die·sel
diet
die-tary

di·eti-tian
diets
dif·fer
dif·fer-ence
dif·fer-ences

dif·fer-ent
dif·fer-en-tial
dif·fer-en-tials
dif·fer-en-tia·tion
dif·fer-ently

dif-fer·ing
dif-fers
dif·fi-cult
dif·fi-cul-ties
dif·fi-culty

dig
di·gest
di·gested
di·gest-ing
dig·ger

dig-ging
*dig·ni-fied
dig·ni-tary
dig·ni-ty
digs

*di·lapi-dated
dila-tory
*di·lemma
dili-gence
dili-gent

dili-gently
di·lute
di·luted
dim
dime

di·men-sion
di·men-sional
di·men-sions
di·min-ish
di·min-ished

dimi-nu-tion
din·ers
di·nettes
din·ing
din·ner

din-ners
din·ner-ware
dio-cese
dip
diph-the·ria

di·ploma
di·plo-macy
di·plo-mas
dip-ping
dire

di·rect
di·rected
di·rect-ing
di·rec-tion
di·rec-tional

di·rec-tions
di·rec-tive
di·rectly
di·rec-tor
di·rec-to·ries

di·rec-tors
di·rec-tory
di·rects
dirt
dirty

disa·bili-ties
disa-bil·ity
dis-abled
dis·ad-van-tage
dis·ad-van-tages

disa-gree
*disa·gree-able
disa·gree-ment
dis·al·low-ance
dis·al-lowed

dis·ap-pear
dis·ap·pear-ance
dis·ap-peared
dis·ap·pear·ing
dis·ap-pears

dis·ap-point
dis·ap-pointed
dis·ap-point·ing
dis·ap·point-ment
dis·ap·point-ments

dis·ap-proval
dis·as·so-cia-tion
dis-as·ter
dis-as-ters
dis·as-trous

dis-banded
dis-burse
dis-bursed
dis-burse-ment
dis·burse-ments

dis-burs·ing
disc
dis-calm·ing
dis-card
dis-carded

*dis·cern-ible
dis-charge
dis-charged
dis-charges
dis-charg·ing

dis·ci·ple-ship
*dis·ci-pline
dis-close
dis-closed
dis-closes

dis-clos·ing
dis-clo-sure
dis-color
dis·com-fort
dis·com-forts

*dis·con-cert
dis·con-nect
dis·con-nected
dis·con-nect·ing
dis·con-tinu-ance

dis·con-tinue
dis·con-tin·ued
dis·con-tin·ues
dis·con-tinu·ing
*dis-cord

dis-count
dis-counted
dis-count·ing
dis-counts
dis-cour·age

dis-cour-aged
dis·cour-ag·ing
*dis-course
dis-cour-tesy
dis-cover

dis-cov-ered
dis-cov-er·ies
dis-cov-er·ing
dis-cov·ers
dis-cov·ery

*dis-credit
dis-crep-an-cies
dis-crep-ancy
dis-cre-tion
dis-cre-tion·ary

dis-crimi-nate
dis-crimi-nat·ing
dis-crimi-na-tion
dis-crimi-na-tory
dis-cuss

dis-cussed
dis-cusses
dis-cuss·ing
dis·cus-sion
dis·cus-sions

dis-ease
dis-eased
dis-eases
*dis·grace-ful
*dis·guise

dis-gusted
dish
dishes
*dis-hon·est
dis-hon-esty

dis·in-fec-tant
dis·in·te-gra-tion
*dis·like
dis·lo-ca-tion
dis·lo-ca-tions

*dis-loyal
dis·mem-ber-ment
*dis-missal
dis-missed
dis·or-der

dis·or-ders
dis·or-ga-nized
dis-patch
dis-patched
dis-patcher

dis-patch·ers
dis-patch·ing
dis·pel
dis·pen-sary
dis-penser

dis-placed
dis-place-ment
dis-play
dis-played
dis-player

dis-play·ing
dis-plays
dis-plea·sure
dis·pos-able
dis-posal

dis·pos-als
dis-pose
dis-posed
dis-pos·ing
dis-po-si-tion

dis·pos-sessed
*dis·pro-por-tion·ate
dis-pute
dis-puted
dis-putes

dis-qual·ify
dis·re-gard
dis·re-garded
dis·re-spect
dis·rup-tion

dis·rup-tions
dis·sat-is-fac-tion
dis·sat-is-fied
dis-sect·ing
dis·semi-nate

dis·semi-nated
dis·ser-ta-tion
dis·ser-ta-tions
dis·ser-vice
dis·simi·lar

dis·si-pated
dis·si-pator
*dis·so-lu-tion
dis-solve
dis-solved

dis-solves
dis-solv·ing
dis-tance
dis-tances
dis-tant

dis-taste·ful
dis-tilled
dis-till·ery
dis-tinct
dis·tinc-tion

dis·tinc-tions
dis·tinc-tive
dis·tinc-tive-ness
dis-tinctly
dis-tin-guish

dis·tin-guished
dis-tort
dis-torted
dis-tract·ing
dis-tress

dis-tressed
dis-tress·ing
dis-trib·ute
dis-trib-uted
dis-trib-utes

dis-trib-ut·ing
dis·tri-bu-tion
dis·tri-bu-tions
dis·tribu-tive
dis·tribu·tor

dis-tribu-tors
dis·tribu·tor-ship
dis-trict
dis-tricts
dis-trust·ful

dis-turb
dis-tur-bance
dis-turbed
dis-turb-ing
ditch

ditches
ditto
di-verse
di-ver-si-fi-ca-tion
di-ver-si-fied

di-ver-sify
di-ver-sion
di-ver-sity
di-verted
di-vide

di-vided
divi-dend
divi-dends
di-vider
di-vid-ers

di-vides
di-vine
div-ing
di-vin-ity
di-vi-sion

di-vi-sional
di-vi-sions
di-vorce
di-vorced
di-vor-cees

di-vulged
do
dock
docket
doc-tor

doc-toral
doc-tor-ate
doc-tors
doc-trine
doc-trines

docu-ment
docu-men-tary
docu-men-ta-tion
docu-ment-ing
docu-ments

dodge
does
doesn't
doffed
dog

dogs
doing
doll
dol-lar
dol-lars

doll-ies
dol-phin
dome
do-mes-tic
do-mes-ti-cally

do-mes-tics
do-mi-cile
do-mi-ciled
do-mi-cili-ary
domi-nate

domi-nated
domi-na-tion
*domi-neer-ing
do-nate
do-nated

do-nat-ing
do-na-tion
do-na-tions
done
donor

do-nors
don't
door
door-bell
door-knob

doors
*dor-mant
dor-mi-to-ries
dor-mi-tory
dose

dot
dots
dou-ble
dou-bled
dou-bles

dou-bling
dou-bloons
dou-bly
doubt
doubted

doubt-ful
doubt-less
doubts
dough-nuts
dove-tail

dowel
down
down-hill
down-ing
down-right

down-stream
down-swing
down-town
down-trend
down-ward

dozen
doz·ens
drab
draft
drafted

draft-ing
drafts
drafts-man
drag
drag-ging

dragon
drain
drain-age
drained
drains

dra-matic
drama-tized
drap-er·ies
drapes
dras-tic

dras·ti-cally
draw
draw-back
drawer
draw-ers

draw-ing
draw-ings
drawn
dread
dread-ful

dream
dreamed
dreams
dredg-ing
dress

dressed
dresser
dress-ers
dresses
dress-ing

dress-ings
drew
dried
drier
drift

drifted
drill
drilled
drill-ing
drills

drink
drink-ing
drinks
drip
drive

driven
driver
driv-ers
drives
drive-way

drive-ways
driv-ing
drop
dropped
drop-ping

drops
drought
drouth
drove
*drowsy

drudge
drudg-ery
drug
drug-gist
drug-gists

drugs
drug-store
drum
drums
drunk

drunken
dry
dryer
dry·ers
dry·ing

dual
*du·bi-ous
duck
ducks
duc-tile

ducts
due
dues
dug
duke

dull
duly
dummy
dump
dumped

dump- ing
dun
dun- ga·ree
dun- ga- rees
duns

du·pli- cate
du·pli- cated
du·pli- cates
du·pli- cat·ing
du·pli- ca- tion

du·pli- ca·tor
du·pli- ca- tors
du·ra- bil·ity
du·ra- ble
du·ra- tion

du·ra- tions
*du·ress
dur·ing
dust
dust- less

du·ties
duty
dwell- ing
dwell- ings
*dwin- dle

dye
dyed
dye·ing
dyers
dy·namic

dy·nam- ics

E

each
eager
ea·gerly
ear
ear- lier

ear- li·est
early
ear- marked
ear- mark·ing
earn

earned
earner
earn- ers
ear- nest
ear- nestly

earn- ing
earn- ings
earns
ear- phone
ear- phones

ear- piece
ear- rings
ears
earth
earth·en- ware

earth- quake
earth- quakes
ease
easel
ease- ment

eas·ier
eas- iest
eas·ily
eas·ing
east

eas- terly
east- ern
east- wardly
easy
eat

eaten
eat·ers
eat·ing
eats
ebony

echo
echo- ing
econo- met·ric
eco- nomic
eco- nom- ical

eco·nomi- cally
eco- nom·ics
econo- mies
econo- mist
econo- mists

econo- mize
econo- miz·ing
econ- omy
ecu·men- ical
edge

edges
edg·ing
ed·ible
edit
ed·ited

ed·it-ing
edi-tion
edi-tions
edi·tor
edi·to-rial

edi·to-ri·ally
edi·to-ri·als
edi-tors
edu-cate
edu-cated

edu·cat-ing
edu·ca-tion
edu-ca-tional
edu·ca-tion-ally
edu·ca-tions

edu·ca-tor
edu·ca-tors
ef·fect
ef·fected
ef·fect-ing

ef·fec-tive
ef·fec-tively
ef·fec-tive-ness
ef·fects
ef·fi-cacy

ef·fi-ciency
ef·fi-cient
ef·fi-ciently
ef·flu-ent
ef·fort

ef·fort-less
ef·fort-lessly
ef·forts
egg
egg·nog

eggs
*ego-tist
eight
eigh-teen
eigh-teenth

eighth
eighty
eighty–three
ei·ther
eking

elabo-rate
elabo·ra-tion
elapse
elapsed
elas-tic

*elas-tic·ity
el·bow-room
elder
el·derly
elect

elected
elect-ing
elec-tion
elec-tions
elec-tive

elec-tives
elec-tor·ate
elec-tric
elec·tri-cal
elec·tri-cally

elec·tri-cian
elec·tri-cians
elec-tric·ity
elec-trics
elec·tri-fi-ca-tion

elec-tron
elec-tronic
elec-tron·ics
elec-tros
elec·tro-static

ele-gant
ele-ment
ele-men·tary
ele-ments
ele-phant

ele-vate
ele-vated
ele-vat·ing
ele-va-tion
ele-va-tions

ele-va·tor
ele-va-tors
eleven
elev-enth
elic-ited

eli·gi-bil·ity
eli·gi-ble
eli·gi-bles
elimi-nate
elimi-nated

elimi-nates
elimi·nat-ing
elimi·na-tion
elite
elm

elms
*elo-quence
else
else's
else-where

em·bank-ment
em·bar-goes
em·bark
em·bar-rassed
em·bar-rass·ing

em·bar-rass-ment
em·bassy
*em·bez-zle-ment
em·blem
em·blems

em·bod-ied
em·bossed
em·brace
em·braced
em·broil-ment

em·bryo
em·er-alds
emerge
emer·gen-cies
emer-gency

emery
emi-nently
emmer
emo-tional
emo·tion-ally

emo-tions
em·pha-sis
em·pha-size
em·pha-sized
em·pha-sizes

em·phati-cally
em·phy-sema
em·pire
em·ploy
em·ployed

em·ployee
em·ploy-ees
em·ployer
em·ploy-ers
em·ploy-ing

em·ploy-ment
em·ploys
emp-tied
emp-ties
empty

emp·ty-ing
*emu-late
emul·si-fied
emul-sion
en·able

en·abled
en·ables
ena-bling
en·acted
en·ac-tion

en·act-ment
enamel
en·camp-ment
en·cased
en·close

en·closed
en·clos-ing
en·clo-sure
en·clo-sures
en·cod-ing

en·com-pass
en·com-pass·ing
en·coun-ter
en·coun-tered
en·coun-ter·ing

en·cour-age
en·cour-aged
en·cour-age-ment
en·cour-ages
en·cour-ag·ing

en·croach-ment
en·cy·clo-pe·dia
end
en·dan-ger
en·dan-ger·ing

en·deavor
en·deav-ored
en·deav-or·ing
en·deav-ors
ended

end·ing
end-less
en·dorse
en·dorsed
en·dorse-ment

en·dorse-ments
en·dors-ing
endow
en·dowed
en·dow-ment

en·dow-ments
ends
*en·dur-able
*en·dur-ance
en·dure

en·dur-ing
ene-mies
enemy
en·er-getic
en·er·geti-cally

en·er-gies
en·er-gized
en·ergy
en·force
*en·force-able

en·forced
en·force-ment
en·forc-ing
en·gage
en·gaged

en·gage-ment
en·gage-ments
en·gag-ing
en·gen-der
en·gen-dered

en·gine
en·gi-neer
en·gi-neered
en·gi-neer-ing
en·gi-neers

en·gines
en·graved
en·graver
en·grav-ings
*en·gross-ing

en·hance
en·hanced
en·hances
en·hanc-ing
en·joined

enjoy
en·joy-able
en·joyed
en·joy-ing
en·joy-ment

en·joys
en·large
en·larged
en·larg-ing
en·light-en-ing

en·light-en-ment
en·list
en·listed
en·listee
en·list-ing

en·list-ment
enolo-gist
*enor-mity
enor-mous
enor-mously

enough
en·rich
en·rich-ment
en·roll
en·rolled

en·roll-ees
en·roll-ment
en·roll-ments
en·route
en·sem-ble

en·shrined
en·su-ing
en·sure
en·tail
en·tailed

en·tails
en·tan-gle-ments
enter
en·tered
en·ter-ing

en·ter-prise
en·ter-prises
en·ter-pris·ing
en·ters
en·ter-tain

en·ter-tained
en·ter-tainer
en·ter-tain·ers
en·ter-tain·ing
en·ter-tain-ment

en·thused
en·thu-si·asm
en·thu-si·asms
en·thu-si·ast
en·thu-si-as·tic

en·thu-si-as-ti·cally
en·tice-ment
en·tire
en·tirely
en·tirety

en·ti-tle
en·ti-tled
en·ti-tles
en·ti-tling
en·tity

en·trance
en·trances
*en·treat
en·trees
*en·tre-pre-neur

en·tre-pre-neurs
en·tries
en·trusted
en·trust-ing
entry

enu-mer-ated
enun-ci-ate
en-ve-lope
en-ve-lopes
en-vi-able

*en-vi-ous
en-vi-ron-ment
en-vi-ron-mental
en-vi-rons
en-vi-sioned

envy
epi-demic
epi-dem-ics
epi-sode
ep-ochal

epoxy
ep-si-lon
ep-si-lons
equal
equaled

equal-ity
equali-za-tion
equal-ize
equal-ized
equal-izes

equal-iz-ing
equally
equals
equa-tion
*equi-lib-rium

equip
equip-ment
equip-ments
equipped
equip-ping

eq-ui-ta-ble
eq-ui-ta-bly
eq-uity
equiva-lence
equiva-lent

equivo-cal
era
eradi-cate
erase
erased

eraser
eras-ing
era-sure
era-sures
erect

erected
erect-ing
erec-tion
erode
ero-sion

er-rati-cally
er-ro-ne-ous
er-ro-ne-ously
error
er-rors

*erup-tion
es-cala-tion
*es-ca-pade
es-caped
es-cheats

es-cort
es-crow
es-crows
es-pe-cial
es-pe-cially

*es-pio-nage
es-quire
es-quires
es-sence
es-sen-tial

es-sen-tially
es-sen-tials
es-tab-lish
es-tab-lished
es-tab-lishes

es-tab-lish-ing
es-tab-lish-ment
es-tab-lish-ments
es-tate
es-tates

es-teem
es-teemed
es-ti-mate
es-ti-mated
es-ti-mates

es-ti-mat-ing
es-ti-ma-tion
etch-ings
eter-nal
ethe-real

eth-ical
ethi-cally
eth-ics
*eti-quette
*eu-lo-gize

eu-reka
*evacu-ation
evad-ers
evalu-ate
evalu-ated

evalu·at-ing
evalu-ation
evalu-ations
*evapo-rate
*evapo-ra·tion

*eva-sive
even
eve-ning
eve-nings
evenly

event
events
even-tual
even·tu·ally
ever

every
ev·ery-body
ev·ery-day
ev·ery-one
ev·ery-one's

ev·ery-thing
ev·ery-where
evi-dence
evi-denced
evi-dences

evi·dent
evi·den-ti·ary
evi-dently
evil
evinced

evo·lu-tion
evolved
ewes
exact
ex·act-ing

ex·actly
*ex·ag-ger·ate
ex·ag-gera-tion
ex·ami-na-tion
ex·ami-na-tions

ex·am-ine
ex·am-ined
ex·am-iner
ex·am-in·ers
ex·am-in·ing

ex·am-ple
ex·am-ples
exams
*ex·as-per·ate
*ex·as-per-ated

ex·ca-va-tion
ex·ceed
ex·ceeded
ex·ceed-ing
ex·ceed-ingly

ex·ceeds
excel
ex·celled
ex·cel-lence
ex·cel-lency

ex·cel-lent
ex·cel-lently
ex·cel-sior
ex·cept
ex·cepted

ex·cept-ing
ex·cep-tion
ex·cep-tional
ex·cep-tion-ally
ex·cep-tions

ex·cerpt
ex·cerpts
ex·cess
ex·ces-sive
ex-chairman

ex·change
ex·change-able
ex·changed
ex·changes
ex·chang-ing

ex·cise
ex·cite-ment
ex·cit-ing
ex·cit-ingly
ex·clude

ex·cluded
ex·cludes
ex·clud-ing
ex·clu-sion
ex·clu-sions

ex·clu-sive
ex·clu-sively
ex·cur-sion
ex·cus-able
ex·cuse

ex·cused
ex·cuses
exe-cute
exe-cuted
exe·cu-tion

exe·cu-tions
ex·ecu-tive
ex·ecu-tives
ex·ecu-tor
ex·ecu-tors

ex·em-plary
ex·em·pli-fies
ex·em-plify
ex·empt
ex·empted

ex·empt-ing
ex·emp-tion
ex·emp-tions
ex·er-cise
ex·er-cised

ex·er-cises
ex·er-cis·ing
exert
ex·erted
ex·ert-ing

*ex·er-tion
ex·haust
ex·hausted
ex·haus-tive
ex·hibit

ex·hib-ited
ex·hib-it·ing
*ex·hi-bi-tion
ex·hibi-tor
ex·hib-its

exist
ex·isted
ex·is-tence
ex·ist-ing
ex·ists

exit
*ex·on-er·ate
*ex·or-bi-tant
ex·pand
ex·panded

ex·pand-ing
ex·panse
ex·pan-sion
ex·pan-sion·ary
ex·pan-sions

ex·pa-tia-tions
ex·pect
ex·pec-tancy
ex·pec-ta-tion
ex·pec-ta-tions

ex·pected
ex·pect-ing
ex·pects
*ex·pe-di-ency
ex·pe-di-ent

ex·pe-dite
ex·pe-dited
ex·pe-di-tion
ex·pe-di-tions
ex·pe-di-tiously

ex·pend-able
ex·pended
ex·pend-ing
ex·pendi-ture
ex·pendi-tures

ex·pense
ex·penses
ex·pen-sive
ex·pe-ri-ence
ex·pe-ri-enced

ex·pe-ri-ences
ex·pe-ri-enc·ing
ex·peri-ment
ex·peri-men·tal
ex·peri-men-ta-tion

ex·peri-ment·ing
ex·peri-ments
ex·pert
ex·per-tise
ex·pertly

ex·perts
ex·pi-ra-tion
ex·pi-ra-tions
ex·pire
ex·pired

ex·pires
ex·pir-ing
ex·plain
ex·plained
ex·plain-ing

ex·plains
ex·pla-na-tion
ex·pla-na-tions
ex·plana-tory
ex·plicit

ex·plic-itly
ex·plod-ing
*ex·ploit
ex·ploit-ing
ex·plo-ra-tion

ex·plora-tory
ex·plore
ex·plored
ex·plor-ers
ex·plor-ing

ex·plo-sion
ex·plo-sive
ex·port
ex·ported
ex·port-ers

ex·port-ing
ex·ports
ex·posed
ex·po-si-tion
ex·po-sure

ex·press
ex·pressed
ex·presses
ex·press-ing
ex·pres-sion

ex·pres-sions
ex·pres-sive
ex·pressly
ex·press-way
ex·qui-sitely

ex·tend
ex·tended
ex·tend-ing
ex·tends
ex·ten-sion

ex·ten-sions
ex·ten-sive
ex·ten-sively
ex·tent
ex·tenu-at·ing

ex·te-rior
ex·ter-nal
ex·tinct
ex·tin-guish
ex·tin-guisher

ex·tor-tion
extra
ex·tract
ex·tracted
ex·tract-ing

ex·trac-tion
ex·trac-tor
ex·tra-cur·ricu·lar
ex·traor-di-nary
ex·tras

ex·trava-gant
ex·treme
ex·tremely
ex·tru-sion
eye

eyed
eyes
eye-sav·ing
eye-sight

F

fable
fab·ric
fab·ri-cate
fab·ri-cated
fab·ri-ca-tion

fab·ri-ca-tors
fab·rics
fabu-lous
face
faced

faces
facet
fac·ets
fa·cili-tate
fa·cili-tat·ing

fa·cili-ties
fa·cil-ity
fac·ing
fac·ings
fac·sim-ile

fact
fac-tion
fac·tor
fac·to-rial
fac·to-ries

fac-tors
fac-tory
facts
fac-tual
fac-tures

fac·ul-ta-tive
fac·ul-ties
fac-ulty
fad
fade

faded
fading
fail
failed
fail-ing

fails
fail-ure
fail-ures
faint
fair

fairer
fair-grounds
fairly
fair-ness
fairs

fair-way
faith
faith-ful
faith-fully
faiths

fake
fall
fal·la·cies
fal·la·cious
fallen

fall-ing
fal·low
falls
false
falsely

fal·si-fy·ing
fame
famed
fa·mil-iar
fa·mil-iar·ity

fa·mil-iar·ize
fa·mil-iar-iz·ing
fami-lies
fam-ily
fam·ine

fa·mous
fan
*fa·nat-ical
fan-ci·ers
fan-cies

fancy
*fan-fare
fans
fan·ta-sies
fan·tas·tic

far
*farce
fare
fares
*fare-well

*far-fetched
farm
farmed
farmer
farm-ers

farm-ing
farms
far-sighted
far-ther
fas·ci-nated

fas·ci-nat·ing
fas·ci-nat-ingly
fash-ion
fash-ion-able
fash-ioned

fash-ions
fast
fas-ten·ers
faster
fast-est

fat
fatal
fa·tali-ties
fate
fa·ther

fa·ther-land
fa·thers
fa·tigue
fatty
fault

faulted
faults
faulty
favor
fa·vor-able

fa·vor-ably
fa·vored
fa·vor-ing
fa·vor-ite
fa·vor-ites

fa·vor-it·ism
fa·vors
fear
fear-ful
fears

fea·si-bil·ity
fea-si·ble
feast
feat
feath·er-weight

fea-ture
fea-tured
fea-tures
fea-tur·ing
fed

fed-eral
fed·er-ally
fed·er-ated
fed·era-tion
fee

fee·ble
feed
feed-back
feed-ers
feed-ing

feeds
feel
feel-ing
feel-ings
feels

fees
feet
fell
fel·low
fel·low-man

fel-lows
fel·low-ship
fel·low-ships
*fel·ony
felt

felts
fe·male
fe·males
*femi-nine
fen

fence
fences
fenc-ing
fender
fer-mented

fe·ro·cious
fer·ric
fer-tile
fer·tili-za-tion
fer·til-izer

fer·til-iz·ers
fer-vent
fes·ti-val
fes-tive
fever

few
fewer
*fi·ancé
fiber
fi·ber-board

fi·ber-glass
fi·bers
*fic-tional
*fic·ti-tious
fi·del-ity

fid-gety
fi·du-ci·ary
field
fields
fif-teen

fif-teenth
fifth
fif·ti-eth
fifty
fifty–eight

fifty–two
fight
fight-ers
fight-ing
fights

fig·ure
fig-ured
fig-ures
figu-rines
figu-ring

file
filed
filer
files
fil·ing

fill
filled
filler
fill-ers
fill-ing

fills
film
films
film-strip
film-strips

fil·ter
fil-ters
final
fi·nale
fi·nal-ize

fi·nal-ized
fi·nally
fi·nals
fi·nance
fi·nanced

fi·nances
fi·nan-cial
fi·nan-cially
*fin·an-cier
fi·nanc-ing

finch
find
finder
find-ing
find-ings

finds
fine
fined
finer
fines

fin·est
fin·ger
fin-gers
fin·ger-tip
fin·ger-tips

finis
fin·ish
fin-ished
fin·ish-ers
fin-ishes

fin·ish-ing
fir
fire
fire-arms
fired

fire-man
fire-place
fire-places
fire-proof
fires

fire-works
fir·ing
fir-ings
firm
firmer

firmly
firms
first
first-hand
firth

fis·cal
fish
fish·er-ies
fish·er-man
fish·er-men

fish-ery
fish-ing
fis-tula
fis·tu-lae
fit

fit-ness
fits
fit·ted
fit-ting
fit-tings

five
five-eighths
fives
fix
fixed

fix·ing
fix-ture
fix-tures
flag
fla-grant

flags
flair
flames
flam-ing
fla-mingo

flange
flanger
flanges
flan-nel
flan-nels

flap
flaps
flash
flasher
flashes

flash-ing
flash-ings
flat
flatly
flat-tered

flat-ware
fla·vor
fla-vors
flaw
flax

flax-seed
fleet
fleet-ing
flesh
flew

flexi-bil·ity
flex-ible
flex-ing
flex-ural
fli·ers

flight
flights
fling
flip
float

floa·ta-tion
floater
float-ing
flock
flocks

flood
flooded
flood-ing
flood-light
flood-lights

flood-plains
floods
flood-wa·ter
floor
floored

floor-ing
floors
flop
flo-ral
flo-rists

flour
*flour-ish
flow
flow-age
flower

flow-ers
flow-ing
flows
fluc·tu-at·ing
flu-ency

flu-ently
fluffy
fluid
flu·ids
fluo·res-cent

fluo-rine
flush
flushed
fly
flyer

fly·ers
fly·ing
foam
foamed
focal

focus
fo·cused
fo·cus-ing
foe
foil

fold
folded
folder
fold-ers
fold-ing

fo·li-age
folio
folk
folks
fol-lies

fol·low
fol-lowed
fol·low-ers
fol·low-ing
fol-lows

follow–up
follow–ups
fond
fondly
food

foods
food-stuffs
fool-ish
foot
foot-age

foot-ball
foot-hills
foot-ings
foot-prints
foot-steps

foot-wear
for
for·bear-ance
for·bid
for·bid-den

force
forced
*force-ful
for-ceps
forces

forc-ibly
forc-ing
fore-armed
fore-cast
fore-casted

fore-cast·ers
fore-cast·ing
fore-casts
fore-clo·sure
forego

fore-go·ing
fore-ground
*fore-head
for-eign
for-eigner

fore-man
fore-most
fore-noon
fore-see
fore-see-able

fore-seen
fore-sees
fore-sight
fore-sighted
for·est

fore-stall
for-estry
for-ests
for-ever
fore-warn-ing

for-feited
forge
forged
forg-er-ies
for-get

for-get-ting
forg-ing
for-give
for-got
for-got-ten

fork
forks
*for-lorn
form
for-mal

for-mal-ize
for-mally
for-mat
for-ma-tion
formed

former, n.
for-mer, adj.
for-merly
*for-mi-da-ble
form-ing

forms
for-mula
for-mu-las
for-mu-late
for-mu-lated

for-mu-lat-ing
for-mu-la-tion
*for-sake
fort
forth

forth-com-ing
forth-with
for-ti-fied
for-ti-fies
*for-ti-tude

for-tu-nate
for-tu-nately
for-tune
for-tunes
forty

forty–eight
forty–five
forty–one
forty–seven
forty–three

forum
fo-rums
for-ward
for-warded
for-warder

for-ward-ers
for-ward-ing
for-wards
fos-ter
fos-ter-ing

fought
foul
found
foun-da-tion
foun-da-tions

founded
founder
found-ers
found-ing
foundry

foun-tain
four
four–fifths
four-fold
four-teen

fourth
fourthly
fourths
fox
frac-tion

frac-ture
frag-ile
*frag-ment
frag-ments
fra-grance

frame
framed
frames
frame-work
fram-ing

fran-chise
fran-chised
frank
franked
frank-furt-ers

frankly
fran-ti-cally
fra-ter-nal
fra-ter-nity
fra-ter-nity's

fraud
fraudu-lent
fraught
free
freed-man

free-dom
free-ing
freely
free-way
freeze

freezes
freez-ing
freight
freighter
freight-ing

freights
fre-quen-cies
fre-quency
fre-quent
fre-quently

fresh
fresh-man
fresh-men
fric-tion
friend

friend-less
friendly
friends
friend-ship
friend-ships

frieze
fright-ened
frills
fringe
*fri·vol-ity

*frivo-lous
fro
from
front
fronts

frost
frosty
fro·zen
fru·gal
*fru-gal·ity

fruit
fruit-ful
frui-tion
fruits
frus-trat·ing

frus·tra-tion
frus·tra-tions
fry·ing
fudge
fuel

fu·el-ing
ful-fill
ful-filled
ful-fill·ing
ful-fill-ment

ful-fills
full
full-est
full—time
fully

fumes
fun
func-tion
func-tional
func-tioned

func-tion·ing
func-tions
fund
fun·da-men·tal
fun·da-men·tàlly

fun·da-men·tals
funded
fund-ing
funds
fu·neral

fun·gi-cides
funny
fur
fur-bearer
fur-bear·ers

fu·ri-ous
fur-loughed
fur-nace
fur-nish
fur-nished

fur-nish·ers
fur-nishes
fur-nish·ing
fur·nish-ings
fur·ni-ture

fur-ther
fur·ther-ance
fur-thered
fur·ther-ing
fur·ther-more

fuse
fuser
fus·ers
fus-ible
fus·ing

fuss
fussy
fu·tile
fu·til-ity
fu·ture

fu·tures

G

---

gab·ar-dines
gable
gad-gets
gage
gain

gained
gain-ing
gains
gal
gala

galax
gale
gall
gal-lant
gal·ley

gal·lon
gal·lon-age
gal-lons
*gall-stone
gals

gal·va-nized
gal·va-niz·ing
gam·ble
gam-bling
game

games
gang
gap
gaps
ga·rage

ga·rages
gar·den
gar-dens
gar·lic
gar-ment

gar-ments
gar-ters
gas
gase-ous
gas-keted

gas-kets
gas-light
gaso-line
gas-tric
gate

gates
gate-way
gate-ways
gather
gath-ered

gath-er·ing
gauge
gauges
gauze
gave

gay
ga·zette
ga·zettes
gaz·ing
gear

geared
gear-ing
gear-less
gears
gel

gela-tin
gems
gen-eral
gen·er-al-ists
gen·er-al-ized

gen·er-ally
gen·er-als
gen·er-ate
gen·er-ated
gen·er-ates

gen·er-at·ing
gen·era-tion
gen·era-tions
gen·era-tor
gen·era-tors

ge·neric
gen·er-os·ity
gen·er·ous
gen·er-ously
*gen·ius

ge·niuses
gen·tle
gen·tle-man
gen·tle-men
gen·tly

gen·try
genu-ine
genu-inely
geo-graphic
geo-graph-ical

G

ge·og-raphy
geo·log-ical
ge·olo-gist
ge·ome-try
geri·at-ric

geri·at-rics
germ
ger-mane
ges-ture
get

gets
get-ting
get–together
gey·ser
*ghastly

ghet-tos
giant
gi·ants
gift
gifted

gifts
*gi·gan-tic
gig-ging
gill
ging-ham

gird
gir·dle
girl
girls
girts

gist
give
given
giv·ers
gives

giv·ing
glad
gladly
glam·or-ized
*glam-or·ous

*glam-our
glance
glanc-ing
glands
*glan-du·lar

glare
glass
glasses
glass-ine
glass-ware

glaze
glaz-ing
gleam-ing
gleaned
glides

glid-ing
glimpse
glis-ten
glis-ten·ing
global

globe
globes
*gloomy
glo-rify
glo-ri·ous

gloss
glossy
glove
gloves
glow-ing

glue
glued
gluer
glu-ing
glut-ting

gnarled
*gnaw-ing
go
go–ahead
goal

goals
gob
god-dess
gods
god-send

goes
going
gold
golden
golf

golf-ing
gon-do·las
gone
good
good-bye

goodly
good-ness
goods
good-will
goose

*gor-geous
gos·sip
got
got·ten
gour-met

gov·ern
gov-erned
gov-ern·ing
gov·ern-ment
gov·ern-men·tal

gov·ern-ments
gov-er·nor
gov-er-nors
gown
gowns

grab
grab-bing
grace
graced
grace-ful

graces
gra·cious
gra·ciously
gra·cious-ness
grade

graded
grader
grades
gra·di-ent
grad-ing

grad-ual
gradu-ally
gradu-ate
gradu-ated
gradu-ates

gradu-at·ing
gradu-ation
gradu-ations
grain
grains

gram
gram-mar
grams
grand
grand-child

grand-fa·thers
grand-moth·ers
grand-par·ents
grands
grange

gran-ite
grant
granted
grant-ing
*grantor

grants
granu-lated
granu-la-tion
grape-vine
graphic

graphi-cally
graph-ite
grap-pling
grasp
grasped

grass
grasses
grass-roots
grate-ful
grate-fully

grate-ful-ness
grati·fi-ca-tion
grati-fied
grati-fy·ing
*gra·tis

grati-tude
gra·tui-ties
grave
gravel
grav-est

grav-ity
gray
graz-ing
grease
greases

great
greater
great-est
greatly
great-ness

greats
*greedy
green
greet
greet-ing

greet-ings
*gre-gari·ous
grew
grey-hound
*griev-ance

grieved
grill
grills
grim
grind

grind-ing
grip
grip-per
grips
grit

grit-ting
gro·cer
gro-cers
gro-cery
*groggy

groomed
groove
groover
grooves
gross

grossed
grossly
*gro-tesque
ground
grounds

ground-work
group
grouped
group-ing
groups

grout
grout-ing
grove
*grovel
groves

grow
grower
grow-ers
grow-ing
grown

grows
growth
*grudge
*grue-some
guar-an·tee

guar-an·teed
guar-an-tee·ing
guar-an·tees
guar-anty
guard

guarded
guard-ian
guard-ians
guards
*gu·ber-na-to·rial

guess
*guessed
guest
guests
guid-ance

guide
guided
guide-lines
guide-post
guides

guid-ing
guild
guilty
gui·tar
gulf

gulfs
*gul-li·ble
gulp
gum
gummed

gums
gun
gun-wales
gus·set
gut-ter·ing

guy
guys
gym
gym·na-sium
gym·nas-tics

gyp·sum

H

habit
habi-tat
hab·its
*ha·bit-ual
had

had-dock
hadn't
hail
hailed
hair

haired
hairy
hale
half
*half-back

*half-hearted
half-way
hall
hall-way
hall-ways

halo
halt
halted
halves
ham

ham·mer
ham·mer-ing
ham·mers
hand
hand-bag

hand-book
hand-books
handed
hand-ful
handi-cap

handi-capped
handi-caps
hand-ily
hand·ker-chief
hand·ker-chiefs

han·dle
han·dle-bar
han·dled
han·dles
han·dling

hand-outs
hand-picked
hands
hand-some
hand-somely

hand-writ·ten
handy
handy-man
hang
*hangar

hang-ers
hang-ing
*hap·haz-ard
hap·pen
hap-pened

hap·pen-ing
hap·pen-ings
hap-pens
hap·pen-stance
hap-pier

hap·pi-est
hap-pily
hap·pi-ness
happy
ha·rassed

har·bor
hard
harden
hard-ened
hard-en·ing

harder
hard-est
*hard-hearted
hardly
hard-ship

hard-ships
hard-ware
hard-wood
harm
harm-ful

harm-less
*har·mo·ni·ous
har·mo·ni-ously
har·mo-nizes
har-ness

harp-ist
harsh
har-vest
har-vested
har-vester

har-vest·ing
has
hasn't
has·ten
has-tened

hast-ily
hasty
hat
hatch
hatcher

hatch-ing
hate
*ha·tred
hats
*haughty

haul
hauler
haul-ers
haul-ing
have

ha·vens
haven't
hav·ing
havoc
hawks

hay
hay-wire
haz·ard
haz-ard·ous
haz-ards

*hazy
he
head
head-aches
headed

H

head-ers
head-ing
head-ings
head-lights
head-lines

head-mas·ter
head-quar·ters
heads
healer
health

health-ful
health-ful-ness
health-ier
healthy
hear

heard
hear-ing
hear-ings
hears
*hear-say

heart
heart-aches
*heart-break-ing
heart-ened
heart-felt

hearth-side
heart-ily
hearts
hearty
heat

heated
heater
heat-ers
heat-ing
heav-enly

heav-ier
heav-ily
heavy
heck
he'd

hedge
heeded
*heed-less
heels
height

height-ened
heights
heir
heirs
held

he·lium
he'll
hello
help
helped

helper
help-ers
help-ful
help-fully
help-ful-ness

help-ing
help-less
help-lessly
helps
hem

hemi-sphere
hem·or·rhoids
hen
hence
hence-forth

hens
her
her-alds
herb
her·bi-cides

herd
herds
here
here-af·ter
hereby

*he·redi-tary
*he·red-ity
herein
hereof
here's

heres
*her·esy
hereto
here·to-fore
here-un·der

here-with
heri-tage
her·nia
her·ni-ated
hero

he·roes
he·roic
hers
her-self
he's

*hesi-tancy
hesi-tant
hesi-tate
hesi-tated
het·ero-ge-neous

hex
hi
hia·tus
hick·ory
hid·den

*hide·ous
high
higher
high·est
high—fidelity

high-land
high-light
high-light·ing
high-lights
highly

high-way
high-ways
hikes
hik·ing
*hi·lari·ous

hill
hills
hilly
hilt
him

him-self
hind
hin-dered
hinge
hint

hip
hire
hired
hires
hir·ing

his
his-toric
his·tor-ical
his·tori-cally
his·to-ries

his-tory
hit
hitch
hith-erto
hits

hit-ting
hob-bies
hobby
hod
hoe

hog
hogs
hoist
hold
holder

hold-ers
hold-ing
hold-ings
hold-over
holds

hole
holes
holi-day
holi-days
holly

holo-caust
holt
holy
*hom·age
hom·bre

home
home-com·ing
home-land
home-less
home-like

home-made
home-mak·ing
home-owner
home-own·ers
homes

home-sick
home-stead
home-work
*homi-cide
ho·moge-nized

hon·est
hon-estly
hon-esty
honey
hong

hon·ing
honor
hon·or-able
hon·or-ary
hon-ored

hon·or-ing
hon·ors
hood
*hood-lum
hoo·doo

hoods
hook
hooked
hoot
hop

hope
hoped
hope-ful
hope-fully
hope-less

hope-less-ness
hopes
hop·ing
hop·per
hop-pers

ho·ri-zon
ho·ri-zons
hori-zon·tal
hori-zon-tally
horn

hor-ri·ble
hor·ror
horse
horse-less
horses

horse-shoe
hose
ho·siery
hos-pi·tal
hos·pi-tal·ity

hos·pi·tali-za-tion
hos·pi-tal·ized
hos·pi-tals
host
hos-tile

host-ing
hosts
hot
hotel
ho·tels

hotly
hot·ter
hot-test
hour
hourly

hours
house
house-clean·ing
house-coat
housed

house-hold
house-keep·ing
house-mother
houses
house-wares

house-wife
house-wives
hous-ing
hover
how

howdy
how-ever
how's
*hub·bub
huge

hull
hulls
human
*hu·mane
hu·mani-tar·ian

hu·mani-tar-ians
hu·mani-ties
hu·man-ity
hu·manly
hum·ble

humid
hu·midi-fi-ca-tion
hu·mil-ity
humor
hu·mor-ist

hu·mor-ous
hunches
hun-dred
hun-dreds
hun-dredth

hun·dred-weight
hung
hun·ger
hun-ger·ing
hun·gry

hunt
hunter
hunt-ers
hunt-ing
hur·dle

hur·ri-cane
hur·ri-canes
hur-ried
hurry
hurt

hurt-ful
hurts
hus-band
hus-bands
husky

hus·tle
huts
hy·brid
hy·brid-iz·ers
hy·drant

hy·drants
hy·drau·lic
hydro
hy·dro-car·bon
hy·dro-elec·tric

hy·dro-gen
hy·dro-logic
hy·giene
hymn
hymns

*hyp-no·sis
hy·po-al-ler-genic
*hy·poc-risy
hy·po-der-mics
hy·pothe-sis

hy·po-thy-roid·ism
hys·te-ria
hys-ter-ics

I

I
ice
icer
icing
I'd

id
idea
ideal
ide-al·ism
ide-ally

ide·als
ideas
iden·ti-cal
iden·ti-fi-able
iden·ti-fi-ca-tion

iden·ti-fi-ca-tions
iden·ti-fied
iden·ti-fies
iden-tify
iden·ti-fy·ing

iden-tity
idle
idle-ness
*idol-ize
if

igloo
ig·ni-tion
ig·no-rance
*ig·no-rant
ig·nore

ig·nored
ig·nor-ing
I'll
ill
il·le-gal

*il·le·giti-mate
il·lit-er·acy
il·lit-er·ate
ill-ness
*il·log-ical

il·lu-mi-nated
il·lu-mi-nat·ing
il·lu-sion
il·lus-trate
il·lus-trated

il·lus-trates
il·lus-trat·ing
il·lus-tra-tion
il·lus-tra-tions
il·lus-tra-tive

*il·lus-tri·ous
I'm
image
imagi-na-tion
imagi-na-tive

imag-ine
imag-ined
imag-in-ing
*im·bibe
imi·ta-tion

imi·ta-tions
*im·macu-late
im·ma-te-rial
im·mea-sur·ably
im·me-di-ate

im·me-di-ately
im·mense
im·mensely
im·mi-grant
im·mi-gra-tion

im·mor-tal
*im·mov-able
im·mune
im·mu-nity
im·mu-ni-za-tion

im·pact
im·pacts
im·pair
im·paired
im·pair-ment

im·pair-ments
im·par-tial
*im·passe
im·pa-tient
im·ped-ance

im·pedi-ment
im·pelled
im·pel-ler
im·pend-ing
*im·pene-tra·ble

im·pera-tive
im·per-fect
*im·per-fec-tion
im·pe-rial
*im·petu-ous

*im·pe-tus
im·ple-ment
im·ple-men-ta-tion
im·ple-mented
im·ple-ment·ing

im·ple-ments
im·pli-ca-tions
im·plied
im·plies
*im·plore

imply
im·port
im·por-tance
im·por-tant
im·por-tantly

im·por·ta-tion
im·ported
im·port-ers
im·port-ing
im·ports

im·pose
im·posed
im·poses
im·pos-ing
im·po·si-tion

im·po·si-tions
im·pos-si-bil·ity
im·pos-si·ble
im·pound
im·pound-ment

im·pov-er-ished
*im·prac-ti-ca·ble
im·prac-ti·cal
im·prac-ti-cal·ity
im·preg-na-tion

im·press
im·pressed
im·pres-sion
im·pres-sions
im·pres-sive

im·print
im·printed
im·print-ing
im·pris-oned
im·pris-on-ment

im·prob-able
*im·promptu
im·proper
im·prop-erly
im·prove

im·proved
im·prove-ment
im·prove-ments
im·proves
im·prov-ing

*im·pro-vise
im·pru-dent
im·pulse
in
ina-bil·ity

*in·ac·ces-si·ble
in·ac·cu-ra·cies
in·ac·cu-rate
in·ac-tive
in·ade-qua-cies

in·ade-quacy
in·ade-quate
in·ad·ver-tence
in·ad·ver-tently
in·ad·vis-able

in·ap·pro-pri·ate
in·ar·ticu-late
in·as-much
in·au·gu-ral
in·au·gu-rate

in·au·gu-rated
in·au·gu-rat·ing
in·au·gu-ra-tion
in·board
in·bound

in·can-des-cent
in·cen-tive
in·cen-tives
in·cep-tion
inch

inches
inch-ing
inch-worm
in·ci-dence
in·ci-dent

in·ci-den·tal
in·ci-den-tally
in·ci-dently
in·ci-dents
in·cin-era·tor

in·clem-ent
in·cli-na-tion
in·cli-na-tions
in·clined
in·clud-able

in·clude
in·cluded
in·cludes
in·clud-ing
in·clu-sion

in·clu-sive
*in·co-her·ent
in·come
in·comes
in·com-ing

in·com-pa·ra·ble
*in·com-pe·tence
in·com-pe·tent
in·com-plete
in·com-pletely

*in·com-pre-hen-si·ble
*in·con·ceiv-able
in·con-clu-sive
*in·con-se-quen-tial
in·con-sist·ent

in·con-testa-bil·ity
in·con-ve-nience
in·con-ve-nienced
in·con-ve-nienc·ing
in·con-ve-nient

in·con-vert-ible
in·cor-po-rate
in·cor-po-rated
in·cor-po-rates
in·cor-po-rat·ing

in·cor-po-ra-tion
in·cor-po-ra-tions
in·cor-rect
in·cor-rectly
in·crease

in·creased
in·creases
in·creas-ing
in·creas-ingly
in·cred-ible

in·cre-ment
in·cre-men·tal
in·cre-ments
in·cu-ba·tor
in·cu-ba·tors

in·cum-bent
incur
in·curred
in·cur-ring
in·debted

in·debt-ed-ness
*in·de-cent
in·de-ci-sion
in·de-co-rum
in·deed

*in·de·fen-si·ble
in·defi-nite
in·defi-nitely
in·del-ibly
in·dem-nity

in·de·pen-dence
in·de·pen-dent
in·de·pend-ently
*in·de·scrib-able
*in·de·struct-ible

in·de-ter-mi-nate
index
in·dexed
in·dexes
in·dex-ing

in·di-cate
in·di-cated
in·di-cates
in·di-cat·ing
in·di-ca-tion

in·di-ca-tions
in·dica-tive
in·di-ca-tor
in·di-ca-tors
in·di-cia

in·dict-ment
in·dif-fer-ence
in·dif-fer-ent
in·di-gent
in·di-rect

in·di-rectly
*in·dis-creet
in·dis-crimi-nately
in·dis-pens-able
*in·dis-posed

in·di-vid-ual
in·di-vidu-al·ism
in·di-vidu-al·ity
in·di-vidu-ali-za-tion
in·di-vidu-al-ized

in·di-vidu-ally
in·di-vidu-als
in·doc-tri-nat·ing
*in·do-lence
in·doors

in·duce
in·duce-ments
in·duc-tion
in·dulge
in·dul-gence

in·dulg-ing
in·dus-trial
in·dus-tri-al·ists
in·dus-tri-ali-za·tion
in·dus-tri·ally

in·dus-tries
in·dus-tri·ous
in·dus-try
in·ed-ible
in·ef·fi-cien-cies

in·ef·fi-ciency
in·ef·fi-cient
in·eli-gi·ble
ine·quali-ties
in·eq·ui-ta·ble

in·eq·ui-ties
in·er-tia
in·evi-ta·ble
in·evi-ta·bly
in·ex-cus-able

*in·ex·haust-ible
in·exo-ra·bly
in·ex·pen-sive
in·ex·pen-sively
in·ex·pe·ri-enced

in·fal-li·ble
in·fancy
*in·fan-tile
in·fan-try
in·fants

*in·fatu-ation
in·fected
infec-tion
infer
in·fer-ence

in·fer-ences
in·fe-rior
*in·ferred
in·fes·ta-tion
in·fi-nite

in·fi-nitely
in·fini-tesi-mal
in·fir-mary
in·fir-mity
in·flated

in·fla-tion
in·fla-tion·ary
in·flex-ible
in·flict
in·flu-ence

in·flu-enced
in·flu-ences
in·flu-en-tial
in·flux
in·form

in·for-mal
in·for-mal·ity
in·for-mally
in·for-ma-tion
in·for-ma-tional

in·forma-tive
in·formed
in·form-ing
in·forms
in·frac-tions

in·fra-red
in·fre-quent
in·fringe-ment
in·fringe-ments
in·fused

in·ge-nious
in·ge-nu·ity
in·genu-ous
*in·grati-tude
in·gre-di·ent

in·gre-di·ents
in·gui-nal
in·habi-tants
in·her-ent
in·heri-tance

in·her-ited
*in·hibit
ini-tial
ini-tialed
ini-tially

ini-tials
ini-ti·ate
ini-ti-ated
ini-ti-at·ing
ini·tia-tion

ini·tia-tive
in·ject
in·jec-tion
in·jure
in·jured

in·ju-ries
in·jur-ing
in·ju-ri·ous
in·jury
*in·jus-tice

ink
inked
inks
in·laid
in·land

inlay
inlet
in·lets
in·mate
in·mates

inn
in·nate
inner
in·ner-spring
inn-keep·ers

*in·no-cence
in·nocu-ous
in·no-va-tion
in·no-va-tions
in·nu·mer-able

in·ocu-lat·ing
*in·op·por-tune
in·pa-tient
input
in·quire

in·quired
in·quires
in·qui-ries
in·quir-ing
in·quiry

*in·quisi-tive
in·roads
ins
*in·sa·ti-able
*in·scrip-tion

in·sect
in·sec·ti-cide
in·sec·ti-cides
in·sects
*in·sepa-ra·ble

in·sert
in·sert-able
in·serted
in·sert-ing
in·ser-tion

in·serts
in·side
in·sight
in·sights
in·sig-nifi-cant

*in·sinu-ation
in·sist
in·sist-ing
in·sists
in·so-far

*in·so-lence
in·spect
in·spected
in·spect-ing
in·spec-tion

in·spec-tions
in·spec-tor
in·spec-tors
in·spects
in·spi-ra-tion

in·spi-ra-tional
in·spire
in·spired
in·spir-ing
in·stall

in·stal-la-tion
in·stal-la-tions
in·stalled
in·staller
in·stall-ing

in·stall-ment
in·stall-ments
in·stance
in·stances
in·stant

in·stantly
in·stead
*in·sti-gate
in·sti-gated
in·still

in·sti-tute
in·sti-tuted
in·sti-tutes
in·sti-tu-tion
in·sti-tu-tional

in·sti-tu-tions
in·struct
in·structed
in·struct-ing
in·struc-tion

in·struc-tional
in·struc-tions
in·struc-tive
in·struc-tor
in·struc-tors

in·stru-ment
in·stru-men·tal
in·stru-men-tal·ity
in·stru-men-ta-tions
in·stru-ments

*in·sub·or·di·nate
in·suf·fi·ciency
in·suf·fi·cient
in·su·late
in·su·la·tion

in·sura·bil·ity
in·sur·ance
in·sure
in·sured
in·sureds

in·surer
in·sur·ers
in·sures
in·sur·ing
in·sur·mount·able

in·tact
in·take
in·tan·gi·ble
in·tan·gi·bles
in·te·gral

in·te·grated
in·te·gra·tion
in·teg·rity
in·tel·lect
in·tel·lec·tual

in·tel·li·gence
in·tel·li·gent
in·tel·li·gently
in·tel·li·gi·ble
in·tend

in·tended
in·tend·ing
in·tends
in·tense
in·ten·si·fied

in·ten·si·fier
in·ten·sify
in·ten·sity
in·ten·sive
in·ten·sively

in·tent
in·ten·tion
in·ten·tional
in·ten·tion·ally
in·ten·tions

in·tents
in·ter·act
in·ter·agency
*in·ter·cede
*in·ter·cept

in·ter·change
in·ter·coastal
in·ter·com
in·ter·com·mu·ni·ca·tion
in·ter·cor·po·rate

in·ter·de·nomi·na·tional
*in·ter·de·pen·dence
in·ter·de·pen·dent
in·ter·est
in·ter·ested

in·ter·est·ing
in·ter·ests
in·ter·fac·ing
in·ter·fere
in·ter·fered

in·ter·fer·ence
in·ter·fer·ing
in·terim
in·te·rior
in·te·ri·ors

in·ter·lac·ing
in·ter·leaved
in·ter·line
in·ter·lock·ers
in·ter·me·di·ary

in·ter·me·di·ate
in·ter·me·di·ates
in·ter·mit·tent
in·ter·moun·tain
in·tern

in·ter·nal
in·ter·na·tional
in·ter·na·tion·ally
in·tern·ists
in·tern·ship

in·tern·ships
in·ter·of·fice
in·ter·planted
in·ter·play
in·ter·po·late

in·ter·pret
in·ter·pre·ta·tion
in·ter·pre·ta·tions
in·ter·pre·ta·tive
in·ter·preted

in·ter·pret·ing
in·ter·prets
in·ter·rupt
in·ter·rupted
in·ter·rupt·ing

in·ter·rup·tion
in·ter·scho·las·tic
in·ter·sec·tion
in·ter·sec·tions
in·ter·spersed

in·ter·state
in·ter·val
in·ter·vals
*in·ter·vene
in·ter·ven·ing

in·ter·ven·tion
in·ter·view
in·ter·viewer
in·ter·view·ing
in·ter·views

in·tes·tate
in·ti·macy
in·ti·mate
in·ti·mately
into

*in·tol·er·able
in·tol·er·ance
in·tol·er·ant
in·trac·ta·ble
in·tra·mu·ral

in·tra·state
in·tra·ve·nous
in·tri·cate
in·trigued
in·tri·guing

in·trin·sic
in·tro·duce
in·tro·duced
in·tro·duces
in·tro·duc·ing

in·tro·duc·tion
in·tro·duc·tory
*in·trude
in·tu·bated
*in·tui·tion

in·un·dated
in·vaded
in·vad·ers
in·valid
*in·vali·date

in·val·ided
in·valu·able
in·vari·ably
in·va·sions
in·vented

in·ven·tion
in·ven·tions
in·ven·to·ried
in·ven·to·ries
in·vent·ors

in·ven·tory
in·verse
in·vest
in·vested
in·ves·ti·gate

in·ves·ti·gated
in·ves·ti·gat·ing
in·ves·ti·ga·tion
in·ves·ti·ga·tions
in·ves·ti·ga·tive

in·ves·ti·ga·tors
in·ves·ti·ga·tory
in·vest·ing
in·vest·ment
in·vest·ments

in·ves·tor
in·ves·tors
in·vi·ta·tion
in·vi·ta·tional
in·vi·ta·tions

in·vite
in·vited
in·vites
in·vit·ing
*in·vo·ca·tion

in·voice
in·voiced
in·voices
in·voic·ing
in·vol·un·tary

in·volve
in·volved
in·volve·ment
in·volves
in·volv·ing

*io·dine
ion
ion·iz·ing
iono·sphere
iris

iron
ironed
iron·ers
iron·ing
irons

ir·regu·lar
ir·regu·lari·ties
*ir·rele·vant
*ir·repa·ra·ble
*ir·re·sist·ible

*ir·re·spec·tive
ir·re·spon·si·ble
ir·re·spon·sive
ir·revo·ca·ble
ir·ri·ga·tion

ir·ri-ga-tions
ir·ri-tat·ing
ir·ri-ta-tion
is
is·land

is·lands
isles
isn't
iso-late
iso-lated

iso-lates
iso-la-tion
is·su-ance
issue
is·sued

is·sues
is·su-ing
it
itch
item

itemi-za-tion
item-ize
item-ized
item-iz·ing
items

it·era-tion
itin-er·ary
it's
Its
it·self

I've
ivory
ivy

J

---

jacket
jack-et·ing
jack-ets
jacks
jail

jailed
jammed
jani-tor
jani·to-rial
jar

jar·gon
jars
jaws
*jeal-ous
jeans

jelled
jeop-ar-dize
jeop-ar-dized
jer-seys
jet

jewel
jew-el·ers
jew-elry
jew·els
jig

jin-gling
job
job·ber
job-bers
job-bing

jobs
jockey
jog
jogs
join

joined
join-ing
joins
joint
jointly

joints
joists
joke
joker
jot

jour-nal
jour-nal·ism
jour-nal·ist
jour-nal-is·tic
jour-nals

jour-ney
joy
joy·ful
joy·ous
*ju·bi-lant

ju·bi-lee
judge
judged
judges
judg-ing

judg-ment
judg-ments
u·di-cial
ju·di-ciary
jug

juice
juices
jumbo
jump
jumped

jumper
junc-tion
jun·ior
jun·iors
junk

junk-yard
ju·ries
ju·ris-dic-tion
ju·ris-dic-tional
ju·ris-dic-tions

ju·rist
juror
ju·rors
jury
just

jus-tice
jus·ti-fi·able
jus·ti-fi·ably
jus·ti-fi-ca-tion
jus·ti-fi-ca-tions

jus·ti-fied
jus·ti-fies
jus-tify
justly
ju·ve-nile

ju·ve-niles

K

---

keel
keen
keenly
keep
keeper

keep-ing
keeps
kegs
kept
kero-sene

ket·tle
key
key-board
keyed
key-note

key-punch
key-punch·ing
keys
key-stone
*khaki

kick
kicked
kick-off
kicks
kid

kid·ded
kid-ding
kid·ney
kids
killed

kill-ers
kill-ing
kills
kiln
kilo

kilo-watt
kilo-watts
kind
kin·der-gar·ten
kind-est

kindly
kind-ness
kind-nesses
kin-dred
kinds

king
king-dom
kink
kinker
kink-ing

kit
kitchen
kitch-en-ette
kitch-en-ettes
kitch-ens

kits
knack
knee
knew
knife

knight
knit
knives
knock
knock-down

J

K

knock-ing
knock-outs
knocks
knot
knotty

know
know-ing
knowl-edge
knowl-edge-able
known

knows
*knuckle

L

lab
label
la·bel-ing
labels
labor

labo·ra-to·ries
labo·ra-tory
la·bor-ers
la·bors
labs

laces
lack
lacked
lack-ing
lacks

*lac-quer
lad
lad·der
lad-ders
laden

ladies
lad·ing
lads
lady
laid

lake
lakes
lake-side
lambs
lame

lami-nated
lami-nat·ing
lami-na-tion
lamp
lamps

lamp-shades
land
landed
land-ing
land-ings

*land-lord
land-mark
land-own·ers
lands
land-scape

land-scaped
land-scap·ing
lane
lanes
lan-guage

lan-guages
lan·ing
lan-tern
lap
lapped

lap-ping
lapse
lapsed
lapses
*lar-ceny

large
largely
larger
larg-est
lar·vae

las·sie
last
lasted
last-ing
lastly

lasts
late
lately
later
lat-eral

lat·est
lati-tude
lat·ter
laud-able
laugh

laugh-ter
launch
launched
launches
launch-ing

launch-ings
laun-dered
laun-dries
laun-dry
lava-tory

lav·ish
law
law-fully
lawn
laws

law-suit
law-suits
law-yer
law-yers
lax

lay
lay·ing
lay-men
lay-mens
lay·off

lay-offs
lay-out
lay-outs
lay-over
leach-ing

lead
leader
lead-ers
lead·er-ship
lead-ing

leads
leaf
leaf-let
leaf-lets
league

leagues
leak
leaks
leaky
leaner

lean-ing
learn
learned
learn-ers
learn-ing

lease
leased
lease-hold·ers
leases
leas-ing

least
leather
leath-ers
leave
leaves

leav-ing
lec-ture
lec-turer
lec-tur·ers
lec-tures

led
ledger
ledg-ers
lee·way
left

left–hand
left-overs
leg
le·gal
le·gal-is·tic

le·gal-ity
le·gal-ized
le·gally
leg·end
leg-ible

leg-ibly
leg·is-late
leg·is-lated
leg·is-la-tion
leg·is-la-tions

leg·is-la-tive
leg·is-la·tor
leg·is-la-tors
leg·is-la-ture
leg·is-la-tures

le·giti-mate
legs
leg-umes
lei-sure
lemon

lem·ons
lend
lender
lend-ers
lend-ing

length
lengthen
lengths
length-wise
le·nient

lens
lenses
less
les·see
les-sees

lessen
less-ens
lesser
les·son
les-sons

L

les·sor
les-sors
let
let's
lets

let·ter
let·ter-head
let-ter·ing
let-ters
let-ting

let-tuce
level
lev·eled
lev·els
lever

le·ver-age
le·vers
lev·ied
lev·ies
levy

lia·bili-ties
lia-bil·ity
li·able
li·ai-son
*li·bel-ous

lib-eral
lib·er-ali-za-tion
lib·er-al-ized
lib·er-ally
lib-erty

li·brar-ian
li·brari-ans
li·brar-ies
li·brary
li·cense

li·censed
li·censee
li·cens-ees
li·censes
li·cens-ing

li·cen-sure
licked
lick-ing
lid
lids

lie
lien
liens
lies
lieu

lieu·ten-ant
life
life-long
life's
life-time

lift
lifted
lift-ing
lifts
light

lighted
lighter
light−foot
light-ing
lightly

light-ning
lights
lig-nites
like
liked

like·li-hood
likely
likes
like-wise
lik·ing

limbs
lime
limed
limit
limi·ta-tion

limi·ta-tions
lim-ited
lim-it·ing
lim-it-less
lim·its

limp
lin·den
line
lin·eal
lin·ear

lined
linen
lin·ens
liner
lin·ers

lines
*lin-ge·rie
lin-guis·tic
lin-guis-tics
lin·ing

link
linked
link-ing
links
li·no-leum

lin-seed
lin-tels
lion
lions
lip

liq·uid
liq·ui-date
liq·ui-dated
liq·ui-dat·ing
liq·ui-da-tion

liq·ui-da-tions
liq·ui-da-tor
liq-uids
li·quor
lisle

list
listed
lis·ten
lis-tened
lis-ten·ers

lis-ten·ing
list-ing
list-ings
list-less
lists

lit
lit·er-ally
lit·er-ary
lit·era-ture
litho-graphed

litho-graphic
li·thog-raphy
liti-gate
liti-ga-tion
lit·tle

lit-urgy
live
lived
*live·li-hood
lively

lives
live-stock
liv·ing
load
loaded

loader
load-ing
loads
loaf
loaf-ers

loaf-ing
loan
loaned
loans
lobby

lob-lolly
local
lo·cali-ties
lo·cal-ity
lo·cal-ized

lo·cally
lo·cals
lo·cate
lo·cated
lo·cat-ing

lo·ca-tion
lo·ca-tions
lock
locked
locker

lock-ers
lock-ing
locks
lo·co-mo-tive
lo·co-mo-tives

lodge
lodges
lodg-ing
lodg-ings
log

loges
log·ger
log-ging
logic
log-ical

logi-cally
lo·gis-tics
logo-types
logs
loin

lol·li-pop
lone
*lone·li-ness
lonely
long

long-boat
longer
long-est
long-hand
lon·gi·tu-di·nal

lon·gi·tu-di-nally
longs
look
looked
look-ing

look-out
looks
loop
looped
looper

*loop-hole
loop-holes
loose
loose-leaf
loosen

loos-en-ing
loos-ens
lord
lords
lose

loser
los-ers
loses
los-ing
loss

losses
lost
lot
lots
loud

lounge
lounges
loused
lousy
love

loved
lovely
lover
loves
lov-ing

low
lower
low-ered
low-er-ing
low-est

low-land
lows
loyal
loy-ally
loy-alty

lube
lu-bri-cant
lu-bri-cants
lu-bri-cate
lu-bri-cated

lu-bri-cat-ing
lu-bri-ca-tion
lu-bric-ity
luck
lucky

lu-cra-tive
luff
lug
lug-gage
lum-ber

lum-ber-man
lump
lumpy
lunch
lunch-eon

lunch-eons
lunch-room
lung
lure
lured

lures
lurk
*lus-cious
lush
lus-ter

lus-ter-less
*luxu-ri-ous
lux-ury
lying
lynch

M

---

ma-chine
ma-chin-ery
ma-chines
ma-chin-ing
ma-chin-ists

macki-naw
mad
madam
made
maga-zine

maga-zines
magic
mag-ical
mag-is-trate
mag-is-trates

mag-netic
mag-ni-fi-ca-tion
mag-nifi-cent
mag-nify
mag-ni-tude

ma·hog-any
maid
maids
mail
mail-able

mailed
mailer
mail-ers
mail-ing
mail-ings

mail-room
mails
main
mainly
mains

main-stay
main-tain
main-tained
main-tain·ing
main-tains

main·te-nance
ma·jes-tic
major
ma·jor-ing
ma·jor-lty

ma·jors
make
maker
mak·ers
makes

make-shift
makeup
mak·ing
*mal·ad-just-ment
*ma·laria

male
males
ma·li-cious
mall
mal·nu-tri-tion

malt
mam-moth
man
man·age
man·age-able

man-aged
man·age-ment
man·age-ments
man-ager
mana·ge-rial

man·ag-ers
man-ages
man·ag-ing
man-date
man·da-tory

ma·neu-ver
ma·neu-vered
ma·neu-ver·ing
man·gle
man—hours

*mania
mani-fest
mani·fes-ta-tions
mani-fold
mani-folds

ma·nila
ma·nipu-late
ma·nipu-lat·ing
man-kind
man-kind's

manned
man·ner
*man·ner-ism
man-power
man's

man-sion
man·ual
manu-ally
manu-als
manu-fac-ture

manu-fac-tured
manu-fac-turer
manu-fac-tur·ers
manu-fac-tures
manu-fac-tur·ing

manu-script
many
map
maple
ma·ples

maps
mar
mar-bles
march-ing
mar·ga-rine

mar·gin
mar-ginal
mar-gins
ma·rine
*mari-tal

mark
mark-downs
marked
marker
mark-ers

M

mar·ket
mar·ket-able
mar-keted
mar-ket·ing
mar-ket-ings

mar·ket-place
mar-kets
mark-ing
mark-ings
marks

markup
ma·roon
mar-riage
mar-ried
marry

marsh
mar-shal
mar·vel
mar-vel·ous
mason

*ma·sonry
ma·sons
mass
massed
masses

mas-sive
mast
mas·ter
mas-ter-ful
mas·ter-piece

mas·ter-pieces
mas-ters
mat
match
matched

match-ing
match-less
mate
ma·te-rial
ma·te-ri-al·ize

ma·te-ri-ally
ma·te-ri·als
ma·ter-nity
math
mathe·ma-ti-cian

mathe-mat·ics
mat·ing
ma·tricu-late
ma·tricu-la-tion
*mat·ri-mo-nial

mats
mat·ter
mat-ters
mat-tress
mat-tresses

ma·ture
ma·tured
ma·tures
ma·tur-ing
ma·tu-ri-ties

ma·tu-rity
maxi-mize
maxi-mum
may
maybe

may·on-naise
mayor
may·ors
maze
me

meadow
mea·ger
meal
meals
mean

mean-ing
mean-ing-ful
mean-ing-less
means
meant

mean-time
mean-while
mea·sur-able
mea-sure
mea-sured

mea·sure-ment
mea·sure-ments
mea-sures
mea-sur·ing
meat

meats
me·chanic
me·chan-ical
me·chani-cally
me·chan-ics

mecha-nism
mecha-ni·za-tion
medal
me·dal-lion
media

*me·dian
me·dias
me·dia-tion
me·dia-tor
me·dia-tors

med-ical	mend	mesh
medi-cally	mend-ing	mess
medi-care	men's	mes-sage
medi-cate	men·tal	mes-sages
medi·ca-tion	*men-tal·ity	mes-sen-ger
medi-cen·ter	men-tally	mes-sen-gers
medi-cen·ters	men-tion	met
*me·dici-nal	men-tioned	metal
medi-cine	men-tion·ing	me·tal-lic
medi-cines	men-tions	met·al-lur-gist
*me·dio-cre	menu	met·als
*me·di·oc-rity	mer·can-tile	metal-work·ing
medi-ta-tive	*mer·ce-nary	me·te-oro-log-ical
me·dium	mer·cer-ized	meter
meet	mer·chan-dise	me·ters
meet-ing	mer·chan-dised	method
meet-ings	mer·chan-diser	meth·od-ol·ogy
meets	mer·chan-dis·ing	meth-ods
mel·an-cho·lia	mer-chant	*me·ticu-lous
mel·low	mer-chants	me·ticu-lously
melt	mer·ci-lessly	me·tropo-lis
mem·ber	mer-cury	met·ro-poli-tan
mem-bers	mercy	micro
mem·ber-ship	mere	mi·cro-crys·tals
mem·ber-ships	merely	mi·cro-film
me·mento	mer·est	mi·cro-filmed
memo	merged	mi·cro-film·ing
memo-ra·ble	merger	mi·cro-groove
memo-ran·dum	merg-ers	mi·cro-phone
memo-ran-dums	merit	mi·cro-phones
me·mo-rial	mer-ited	mi·cro-scope
memo-ries	mer·its	mid
mem·ory	mer·ri-est	mid-ci·ties
memos	merry	mid-con·ti·nent
men	mesa	mid-con·ti·nen·tal

mid·day
middle
*middle–aged
mid-dling
mid-dlings

mid-month
mid-night
mid-sea·son
mid-se·mes·ter
midst

mid·way
mid-week
mid-west
mid-west·ern
mid-win·ter

mid-wives
mid-year
might
might-ily
mighty

mi·grate
mild
mile
mile-age
miles

mile-stone
mile-stones
mili-tary
milk
milk-ing

milk-man
milk shakes
mill
mill-ers
mil·li·me·ter

mil·li-nery
mil-lion
mil-lions
mil-lionth
mills

mill-work
mime-ograph
mime-ographed
mime-ograph·ing
mind

minded
*mind-ful
minds
mine
miner

min-eral
min-er-als
mines
mine-sweep·ers
mini-ature

mini-atures
mini-aturi-za-tion
mini-mal
mini-mize
mini-mized

mini-mizes
mini-miz·ing
mini-mum
min·ing
min-is·ter

min-is-ters
min-is·try
mink
minor
mi·nori-ties

mi·nor-ity
mi·nors
min-strel
mints
minus

min·ute, n.
mi·nute, adj.
min-utes
mir-acle
mir-acles

mir·ror
mir-rors
mis·ap-pre-hen-sion
mis·cal-cu-lated
mis·cel-la-neous

mis-chief
*mis·chie-vous
mis·con-cep-tions
mis·count
mis·di-rect·ing

*mis·er-able
mis·ery
mis·for-tune
mis·giv-ings
mis-guided

mis·han-dled
mis·han-dling
mis·hap
mis-haps
mis·in-ter-preted

mis·la-beled
mis-laid
mis-lead
mis·lead-ing
mis·man-ag·ing

mis-matched
*mis·no-mer
mis-place
mis-placed
mis·rep-re-sen-ta-tion

mis·rep-re-sented
mis-routed
miss
missed
misses

mis-sile
mis-siles
miss-ing
mis-sion
mis-sion-ar-ies

mis-sion-ary
mis-sions
mis-spelled
mis-take
mis-taken

mis-tak-enly
mis-takes
mis-ter
mis·tle-toe
misty

mis·un-der-stand·ing
mis·un-der-stand-ings
mis·un-der-stood
mis·used
mite

mi·tered
miti·ga-tion
miti·ga-tive
mix
mixed

mix·ing
mix-ture
mix-tures
mix-up
mob

mo·bile
mo·bil-ity
mo·bi-li-za-tion
mo·bi-liz·ing
moc-ca·sin

mock
mock-ery
mode
model
mod·el-ing

mod·els
mod-er·ate
mod-er-ately
mod-era·tor
mod·ern

mod·erni-za-tion
mod·erni-za-tions
mod·ern-ize
mod·ern-iz·ing
mod·est

mod-estly
modi·fi-ca-tion
modi·fi-ca-tions
modi-fied
modi-fies

mod·ify
modi-fy·ing
*modu-lar
mod·ule
moire

moist-en·ers
mois-ture
mo·las-ses
mold
molded

mold-ing
molds
mole-cules
mole-skin
mom

mo·ment
mo·men-tary
mo·memto
*mo·men-tous
mo·ments

mo·men-tum
mone-tary
money
mon·eys
mon·ies

moni-tor
moni-tored
mon·key
mono-cal-cium
mono-graph

*mo·nopo-lize
mo·nop-oly
*mo·noto-nous
*mon-stros·ity
month

monthly
months
monu-ment
monu-men·tal
monu-ments

mood
moody
moon
moor
moot

mop
mop-ping
mops
moral
mo·rale

mora·to-rium
*mor·bid
more
more-over
morgue

morn-ing
morn-ings
mor-tal·ity
mor·tar
mor-tars

mort-gage
mort-gaged
mort-ga·gee
mort-ga·gees
mort-gages

mort-ga·gor
mort-ga·gors
mor-tu·ary
mos·qui-toes
most

mostly
motel
mo·tels
mother
mother-in-law

moth-ers
moth-proof
moth-proofed
moths
mo·tion

mo·tions
mo·ti-vate
mo·ti-vated
mo·ti-vates
mo·ti-vat·ing

mo·ti-va-tion
mo·ti-va-tional
mo·tive
mo·tives
motor

mo·tor-cy·cle
mo·tor-cy·cles
mo·tor-cy·clists
mo·tor-ing
mo·tor-ist

mo·tor-ists
mo·tor-ized
mo·tors
mould-ing
mount

moun-tain
*moun-tain·ous
moun-tains
mounted
mount-ing

mount-ings
mounts
*mourn-ful
mouse
mouth

mouth-ful
mouth-piece
move
moved
move-ment

move-ments
mover
mov·ers
moves
movie

mov·ies
mov·ing
mow
mowed
mower

mow·ers
mow·ing
much
*mu·ci-lage
mud

muf·fle
mulch
mulch-ing
mule
mules

mul·ti-ple
mul·ti-ples
mul·ti-plied
mul·ti-plies
mul·ti-ply

mul·ti-pur-pose
mul·ti-sec-tion
mul·ti-sheet
mul·ti-sided
mul·ti-tude

mul·ti-tu-di-nous
mul·ti-wall
mul·ti-wave
mul·ti-year
mu·nici-pal

mu·nici-pali-ties
mu·nici-pal·ity
mur-der·ers
*mur-der·ous
mu·ri-atic

*mur-mur·ing
mus-cles
*mus-cu·lar
mu·seum
mu·se-ums

music
mu·si-cal
mu·si-cians
mus·lin
muss

must
*mus-tache
mus-tard
mus-tered
mute

muted
mut·ton
mu·tual
mu·tu-ally
my

my·self
mys-ter·ies
mys-te-ri·ous
mys-tery
mys-ti-fied

mys-ti-fy·ing

N

---

nag
nail
nail-ing
nails
*naive

name
named
namely
name-plate
names

*name-sake
nap-kins
*nar-cotic
nar·ra-tive
nar·row

nary
nasty
na·tion
na·tional
na·tion-ali-za-tion

na·tion-ally
na·tion-als
na·tions
na·tion-wide
na·tive

natu-ral
natu-rali-za-tion
natu-ral-ized
natu-rally
na·ture

na·tures
naval
navi-ga·tor
navy
near

nearby
nearer
near-est
near-ing
nearly

nears
neat
neatly
neb
nec·es-sar·ily

nec·es-sary
ne·ces-si-tate
ne·ces-si-tated
ne·ces-si-tates
ne·ces-si-tat·ing

ne·ces-si-ties
ne·ces-sity
neck
neck-ties
need

needed
need-ing
nee-dle
nee-dles
need-less

need-lessly
needs
needy
nega-tive
nega-tively

N

ne·glect
ne·glected
ne·glect-ing
neg-li-gence
*neg-li-gent

neg-li-gi·ble
ne·go-ti-able
ne·go-ti·ate
ne·go-ti-ated
ne·go-ti-at·ing

ne·go-tia-tion
ne·go-tia-tions
ne·go-tia·tor
neigh-bor
neigh-bor-hood

neigh-bor·ing
neigh-bors
nei-ther
neon
nephew

ner-vous
ner·vous-ness
nest
nest-ing
net

nets
net·ted
net·tle
net-work
*neu-ri·tis

*neu-ro·sis
neu-tral
never
nev·er-the-less
new

new-born
new-comer
new-com·ers
newer
new·est

newly
new-ness
news
news-let·ter
news-let·ters

news-pa·per
news-pa·per-man
news-pa·pers
news-reel
news-stand

news-weekly
next
nib·ble
nice
nicely

nicer
nickel
niece
night
*night-mare

nights
night-time
nil
nine
nine-teen

nine-teenth
ninety
ninth
ni·tro-gen
no

*no·bil-ity
noble
no-body
noel
nog

noise
noise-less
*nois-ily
no·madic
no·men-cla-ture

nomi-nal
nomi-nate
nomi-nated
nomi-nat·ing
nomi-na-tion

nomi-na-tions
nomi-nee
nomi-nees
non-ab-sor-bent
non-ad-mis-si·ble

non-ad-mit·ted
non-al-co-holic
non-as-sess-able
non-cash
non-com-mer-cial

non-com-peti-tive
non-con-fin·ing
*non-con-form·ist
non-con-secu-tive
non-crit-ical

non-disa-bling
non-drink-ing
non-du-pli-cate
non-du-ra·ble
none

none-the-less
non-ex-clu-sive
non-ex-is-tent
non-farm
non-fed-eral

non-for-fei-ture
non-haz-ard-ous
non-im-mi-grant
non-in-ter-fer-ence
non-led-ger

non-mag-netic
non-medi-care
non-mem-ber
non-mem-bers
non-me-tered

non-par-ti-san
non-pay-ment
non-profit
non-re-ceipt
non-re-newal

non-resi-dents
non-re-turn-able
non-rub-ber
non-sched-uled
non-sense

non-sign-ers
non-skid
non-smok-ers
non-stan-dard
*non-stop

non-sub-scriber
non-sub-scrib-ers
non-sur-gi-cal
non-tax-able
non-teach-ing

non-tech-ni-cal
non-trans-fer-able
non-union
non-us-ers
noo-dling

noon
nor
nor-mal
nor-malcy
nor-mally

north
north-east
north-east-ern
north-ern
north-ward

north-west
north-west-ern
nose
not
no-ta-ble

no-ta-rized
no-tary
no-ta-tion
no-ta-tions
note

*note-book
note-books
noted
notes
note-wor-thy

noth-ing
no-tice
no-tice-able
no-ticed
no-tices

no-ti-fi-ca-tion
no-ti-fi-ca-tions
no-ti-fied
no-ti-fies
no-tify

no-ti-fy-ing
not-ing
no-tion
*no-to-ri-ety
no-to-ri-ous

not-with-stand-ing
*nour-ish-ment
nov-el-ties
*nov-elty
*nov-ice

now
nowa-days
no-where
nox-ious
noz-zle

noz-zles
nu-clear
nu-dity
nui-sance
*nul-lify

num-ber
num-bered
num-ber-ing
num-bers
nu-mer-als

nu-mera-tor
nu-meric
nu-mer-ical
nu-mer-ous
nurse

nur-sery
nurses
nurs-ing
*nur-ture
nu-tri-tion

nu-tri-tion-ist
nu-tri-tious
nuts
nut-shell
nylon

ny-lons

O

oak
oaks
oat
oath
oaths

oats
obe-di-ence
obe-sity
obey-ing
obitu-ary

ob-ject
ob-jected
ob-jec-tion
ob-jec-tion-able
ob-jec-tions

ob-jec-tive
ob-jec-tives
*ob-jec-tiv-ity
ob-jects
ob-li-gate

ob-li-gated
ob-li-gates
ob-li-ga-tion
ob-li-ga-tional
ob-li-ga-tions

oblige
obliged
obliger
oblit-er-ate
oblit-er-ated

*oblivi-ous
*ob-nox-ious
oboe
*ob-scene
*ob-scure

ob-ser-vance
ob-ser-va-tion
ob-ser-va-tions
ob-serva-tory
ob-serve

ob-served
ob-serv-ing
*ob-ses-sion
ob-so-les-cence
ob-so-lete

ob-sta-cle
ob-sta-cles
*ob-sti-nate
ob-struc-tion
ob-tain

ob-tain-able
ob-tained
ob-tain-ing
ob-vi-ate
ob-vi-ous

ob-vi-ously
oc-ca-sion
oc-ca-sional
oc-ca-sion-ally
oc-ca-sioned

oc-ca-sions
oc-ci-den-tal
oc-cu-pancy
oc-cu-pant
oc-cu-pa-tion

oc-cu-pa-tional
oc-cu-pa-tions
oc-cu-pied
oc-cu-pies
oc-cupy

oc-cu-py-ing
occur
oc-curred
oc-cur-rence
oc-cur-rences

oc-cur-ring
oc-curs
ocean
o'clock
odd

odds
*odi-ous
odor-less
odors
of

off
*off-color
of-fend
of-fended
of-fend-ers

of·fense
of·fenses
of·fen·sive
offer
of·fered

of·fer·ing
of·fer·ings
of·feror
of·fer·ors
of·fers

off·hand
of·fice
of·fi·cer
of·fi·cers
of·fices

of·fi·cial
of·fi·cially
of·fi·cials
*of·fi·ci·ate
*of·fi·cious

off·set
off·spring
often
of·ten·times
oh

oil
oili·ness
oils
oil·seed
oint·ments

okay
old
older
old·est
old–fashioned

oleo
olive
ol·ives
omi·nous
omis·sion

omis·sions
omit
omits
omit·ted
omit·ting

on
once
one
one–eighth
one–fifth

one–fourth
one–half
one–hundred
one–quarter
*one–self

one–sixteenth
one–sixth
one–tenth
one–third
one–twelfth

oner·ous
ones
only
on·slaught
onto

*opaque
open
opened
opener
open–ers

open–ing
open–ings
openly
opens
opera

op·er·able
op·er·ate
op·er·ated
op·er·ates
op·er·atic

op·er·at·ing
op·era·tion
op·era·tional
op·era·tions
op·era·tive

op·era·tor
op·era·tors
op·er·etta
opin·ion
opin·ions

opos·sum
op·po·nent
op·po·nents
op·por·tune
op·por·tu·ni·ties

op·por·tu·nity
op·pose
op·posed
op·pos·ing
op·po·site

op·po·si·tion
op·po·si·tions
*op·pres·sive
op·ti·cal
op·ti·cally

op·ti·mism
op·ti·mist
op·ti·mis·tic
op·ti·mum
op·tion

op·tional
op·tions
op·tome·try
or
oral

orally
or·ange
or·ange·ade
ora·tor
*ora·tory

orbit
or·bits
or·chard
or·ches·tra
*or·deal

order
or·dered
or·der·ing
*or·der·li·ness
or·derly

or·ders
or·di·nance
or·di·nances
or·di·nar·ily
or·di·nary

ord·nance
organ
or·ganic
or·gan·ist
or·ga·ni·za·tion

or·ga·ni·za·tional
or·ga·ni·za·tions
or·ga·nize
or·ga·nized
or·ga·niz·ers

or·ga·niz·ing
or·gans
ori·ent
ori·en·tal
ori·en·tat·ing

ori·en·ta·tion
ori·ented
ori·gin
origi·nal
origi·nal·ity

origi·nally
origi·nals
origi·nate
origi·nated
origi·nat·ing

origi·na·tor
or·na·men·tal
*or·nate
or·phan
or·phans

or·tho·pe·dic
os·cil·lat·ing
os·cil·la·tion
os·cil·la·tor
*os·ten·ta·tious

other
oth·ers
oth·er·wise
ought
ounce

ounces
our
ours
our·selves
out

out·age
out·ages
*out·board
out·bound
out·break

out·casts
out·come
out·crop·ping
out·dated
outdo

out·door
out·doors
outer
out·er·wear
out·fit

out·fits
out·go·ing
out·ing
out·ings
out·lawed

out·lay
out·lays
out·let
out·lets
out·line

out·lined
out·lines
out·lin·ing
out·lived
out·look

out-ly·ing
out-moded
out-num·bered
out·put
*out-ra-geous

out-reach
out-right
out·run
outs
out·set

out-side
out-sider
out-skirts
out-sold
out-spo·ken

out-stand·ing
out-stand·ingly
out-state
out-wardly
out-weighed

ovens
over
over-age
over-ages
over-all

over-bal·anced
over-bal·ances
over-bid
over-board
over-bur·den

over-charge
over-charged
over-charges
over-come
over-comes

over-com·ing
over-crowded
over-crowd·ing
over-drafts
over-drawn

over-due
over-es·ti·mated
over-ex·pen·di·ture
over-flow
over-flowed

over-flow·ing
over-full
over-haul
over-hauls
over-head

over-in·ven·to·ried
over-joyed
over-land
over-lap
over-lay

over-load
over-loaded
over-long
over-look
over-looked

over-look·ing
overly
over-night
over-paid
over-pay·ment

over-pay·ments
over-print
over-print·ing
over-re·mit·ted
over-ride

over-rid·ing
over-run
over-run·ning
over-save
over-seas

over-sell
over-shadow
over-shad·owed
over-sight
over-sim·pli·fied

over-sim·plify
over-size
over-spend
over-stock
over-stocked

over-stocks
over-sub·scribed
overt
over-throw
over-time

over-weight
over-whelmed
over-whelm·ing
over-whelm·ingly
over-worked

owe
owed
owes
owing
owl

own
owned
owner
own·ers
own·er-ship

own·er-ships
own·ing
owns
ox·fords
oxi·da-tion

oxide
oxi-dizes
oxy·gen
*oys·ter

P

---

pace
pace-set·ter
pa·cific
pack
pack-age

pack-aged
pack-ager
pack-ages
pack-ag·ing
packed

packer
pack-ers
packet
pack-ets
pack-ing

packs
pact
pad
pad·ded
pad-ding

pad·dle
pad-dler
pad-dles
*pad-lock
pad-locks

pads
page
pages
paid
pail

pails
pain
pain-ful
pain-fully
pain-less

pains
*pains-tak·ing
pains-tak-ingly
paint
painted

painter
paint-ers
paint-ing
paint-ings
paints

pair
pairs
pa·ja-mas
pal·ace
pal·at-able

pale
pal·let
pal·leti-za-tion
pal-let-ized
pal-lets

*pal·lor
palm
pal-metto
*pam·per
pam-phlet

pam-phlets
pan
pana-cea
pan-cakes
panel

pan-el·ing
pan-el-ists
pan·els
panic
pan-ning

*pano-rama
pans
*pan·to-mime
pants
paper

pa·per-board
pa·per-hanger
pa·pers
paper work
par

*para-chute
pa·rade
*para-dise
para-dox
para-dox-ical

para-graph
para-graphs
par-al·lel
par-al-lels
*pa·raly-sis

*para-lyze
para-med-ical
*para-mount
*para-phrase
para-ple-gic

*para-site
par-cel
par-cels
par-don
par-don-able

par-ent
par-ent-age
*pa-ren-the-ses
par-ents
par-fait

par-ish
par-ity
park
parked
park-ing

parks
par-lia-men-tar-ian
*par-lia-men-tary
par-lor
par-lors

pa-role
par-son-age
part
*par-take
parted

par-tial
par-tially
par-tici-pant
par-tici-pants
par-tici-pate

par-tici-pated
par-tici-pates
par-tici-pat-ing
par-tici-pa-tion
par-ti-cle

par-ti-cles
par-ticu-lar
par-ticu-larly
par-ticu-lars
par-ties

part-ing
par-ti-tion
par-ti-tioned
par-ti-tions
partly

part-ner
part-ners
part-ner-ship
*par-took
parts

part-time
party
pass
pas-sage
pass-book

pass-books
passed
pas-sen-ger
pas-sen-gers
passes

pass-ing
pas-sive
pass-out
pass-port
past

paste
pasted
pas-tel
*pas-time
pas-tor

pas-tor-ate
pas-try
pas-ture
pas-tured
pas-tures

pat
patch
patched
patch-ing
pate

pat-ent, n.
pa-tent, adj.
pat-ented
pat-en-tee
pat-ents

*pa-ter-nal-ism
path
*pa-thetic
patho-log-ical
pa-tholo-gist

pa-thol-ogy
paths
pa-tience
pa-tient
pa-tients

patio
pa-tri-otic
pa-trol
pa-trol-man
pa-trols

P

pa·tron
pa·tron-age
pa·trons
pat-tern
pat-terned

pat-terns
pat-ting
*pau-city
pause
paved

pave-ment
pa·vil-ion
pav·ing
pay
pay-able

pay-check
pay·day
payee
pay·ing
*pay-master

pay-ment
pay-ments
pay·off
payor
pay-roll

pay-rolls
pays
pea
peace
*peace-able

peace-time
peach
peaches
peak
peaks

pea·nut
pea-nuts
pearl
peat
peb·ble

pecan
*pe·cu-li-ari-ties
pe·cu-ni·ary
pedal
ped·dle

ped·es-tal
pe·des-trian
peel
peel-ing
peer

pekoe
pelts
pen
penal
pe·nal-ize

pe·nal-ized
pen·al-ties
pen-alty
pen-cil
pen-cilled

pen-cils
pend-ing
*pen-du·lum
pene-trant
pene-trate

pene-trated
pene-trat·ing
pene-tra-tion
pen-guin
pen·in-sula

peni-ten-tia·ries
penned
pen-nies
penny
pens

pen-sion
pen-sions
*pen-ta·gon
pent-house
peo-nies

peony
peo·ple
peo-ples
pep
pep·per

pep·per-mint
per
per-ceive
per-cent
per-cent·age

per-cent·ages
per-cent-age-wise
per-cen-tile
*per-cep-tion
per-cep-tive

*per-chance
per·co-la·tor
per-fect
per-fected
per-fect·ing

per-fec-tion
per-fectly
per-fer·vid
per-fidi·ous
per·fo-rated

per·fo·rat·ing
per·fo·ra·tions
per·fo·ra·tor
per-form
per-for-mance

per-for-mances
per-formed
per-former
per-form·ing
per-forms

per-haps
peri-gee
*per·il·ous
per·ils
pe·riod

pe·ri-odic
pe·ri-od-ical
pe·ri-odi-cally
pe·ri-od-icals
pe·ri-ods

peri-scope
per·ish-able
*per-jury
per·ma-nence
per·ma-nent

per·ma-nently
*per-me·ate
per·mis-si·ble
per·mis-sion
per·mis-sions

per·mit
per·mits
per·mit·ted
per·mit·tee
per·mit-tees

per-mit-ting
*per·pen-dicu·lar
per-pet·ual
per-petu·ate
per-plexed

per-plex·ing
per·se-ver-ance
*per·se-vere
per·sis-tence
per·sis-tency

per-sists
per·son
per-sonal
per·son-ali-ties
per·son-al·ity

per·son-al·ize
per·son-al-ized
per·son-ally
*per·soni-fi-ca-tion
per·son-nel

per-sons
per·spec-tive
*per·spi-ra-tion
per-suade
per-suaded

per-sua-sion
per-sua-sive
per·tain
per·tain·ing
per·tains

per-ti·nent
*per-turbed
pe·rusal
pe·ruse
pe·rused

pe·rus-ing
per·va-sive
per·ver-sity
pes·si-mism
*pes·si-mis-tic

pest
pes·ti-cides
pests
pet
pe·tite

pe·ti-tion
pe·ti-tioned
pe·ti-tioner
pe·ti-tions
pe·tro-leum

pe·tro-le·ums
petty
phar-ma-ceu-ti·cal
phar-ma-co-poeia
phar-macy

phase
phases
pheas-ant
phe-nome·nal
phe-nome·non

*phil-an-thropic
*phi·lan-thro-pist
phi-loso-pher
philo-soph·ical
phi-loso-phize

phi-loso·phy
phone
phoned
phon-ing
pho·no-graph

phos-phate
phos-phates
phos-pho-rous
photo
pho-to-copies

pho-to-copy
pho-to-graph
pho-to-graphed
pho-tog-ra-pher
pho-tog-ra-phers

pho-to-graphic
pho-to-graph-ing
pho-to-graphs
pho-tog-ra-phy
pho-ton

pho-tos
pho-to-stat
pho-to-stated
pho-to-static
pho-to-stats

phrase
phrased
phrases
phys-ical
physi-cally

phys-icals
phy-si-cian
phy-si-cians
*physi-cist
phys-ics

physi-ographic
physi-olo-gist
physi-othera-pist
physi-other-apy
*pi-an-ist

piano
pia-nos
pica
pick
picked

picket
pick-et-ing
pick-ing
picks
pickup

pic-nic
pic-nick-ing
pic-nics
pic-to-ri-ally
pic-ture

pic-tured
pic-tures
*pic-tur-esque
pic-tur-ing
pie

piece
pieces
pier
pig
pi-geon

*pi-geon-hole
pig-ment
pig-ments
pig-tail
pike

pile
piled
pil-fer-age
pil-fer-ing
pil-ing

pill
pil-low
pil-lows
pills
pilot

pi-lots
pin
pinch
pine
pine-ap-ple

pines
pink
pin-na-cle
pinned
pin-point-ing

pins
pint
pints
pio-neer
pio-neered

pio-neers
pipe
pipes
pip-ing
piqued

pi-rates
pi-rat-ing
pis-tols
*pis-ton
pis-tons

pit
pitch
pitch-ing
*pit-fall
pit-falls

*piti-ful
pits
pivot
pizza
piz·zas

plac-ard
place
placed
place-ment
place-ments

placer
places
plac-ing
*pla·gia-rism
plagued

plain
plainly
plains
plain-tiff
plain-tiffs

plan
plane
planes
plan-ets
plank-ing

planned
plan-ners
plan-ning
plans
plant

plan·ta-tions
planted
plant-ers
plant-ing
plant-ings

plants
plaque
plaques
plas-ter
plas-tic

plas·ti-cized
plas-tics
plat
plate
pla-teaus

plates
plat-form
plat-ing
plati-num
plats

plat-ted
plat-ting
*plau-si·ble
play
play-boy

played
player
play-ers
play-ground
play-ing

play-rooms
plays
plaza
plea
plead-ing

plead-ings
pleas-ant
pleas-anter
please
pleased

pleases
pleas-ing
plea-sure
plea-sures
pledge

pledged
pledges
pledg-ing
plen-ti·ful
plenty

plier
pli·ers
plight
plots
ploughed

plow
plow-ing
plug
plugged
plug-ging

plugs
plumb-ing
*plump-ness
plunge
plunger

plunges
*plung-ing
plus
ply
ply-wood

pneu-matic
pneu-mo-nia
pocket
pock·et-books
pock-ets

po·etry
poin-set·tia
point
pointed
point-ers

point-ing
points
poi·son
poi-son·ing
poke

poker
pole
poles
po·lice
po·lice-man

poli-cies
pol·icy
poli·cy-holder
poli·cy-hold·ers
polio

pol·ish
pol-ishes
*po·lite-ness
po·lit-ical
po·liti-cally

poli·ti-cians
poli-tics
poll
polled
polls

poll-sters
pol-lu-tion
poly-es·ter
poly-eth-yl·ene
poly-sty-rene

pon-der·ing
pon-der·ous
pool
pools
poor

poorly
pop
pope
pop·lar
pop-overs

pop-pies
poppy
pops
popu-lar
popu-lar·ity

popu-lated
popu-la-tion
popu-la-tions
*popu-lous
*por·ce-lain

porch
porches
pores
pork
port

por-ta·ble
por-ta-bles
por-tage
por·ter
port-fo·lio

port-fo·lios
por-tion
por-tions
*portly
por-tray

por-trayed
por-tray·ing
ports
po·sada
pose

posed
po·si-tion
po·si-tioned
po·si-tions
posi-tive

posi-tively
pos-sess
pos-sesses
pos·sess-ing
pos·ses-sion

pos·ses-sions
pos·ses-sor
pos·si-bili-ties
pos·si-bil·ity
pos·si-ble

pos·si-bly
post
post-age
postal
post-als

post-card
post-cards
posted
poster
*pos·te-rior

post-ers
post-haste
post-holi·day
post-ing
post-man

post-mark
post-marked
post-mas·ter
post-mas·ters
post-paid

post-pone
post-poned
post-pone-ment
posts
post-war

pot
po·ta-toes
po·tency
po·ten-tial
po·ten-tials

pot-pourri
pot·ted
pot-ters
pot-tery
poul-try

pound
pound-ing
pounds
pour
poured

pourer
pour-ing
pov-erty
pow·der
pow-dered

power
pow-ered
pow-er·ful
pow·ers
prac-ti-ca-bil·ity

prac-ti-ca·ble
prac-ti·cal
prac-ti-cally
prac-tice
prac-ticed

prac-tices
prac-tic·ing
prac-ti-tioner
prac-ti-tion-ers
praise

pray
prayer
pray-ers
preach
preach-ers

preach-ing
pre-ad·mis-sion
pre-ap·pli-ca-tion
pre-ar·range
pre-as·sem-bled

pre-au·tho-rized
*pre-cari-ous
pre-cau-tion
pre-cau-tion·ary
pre-cau-tions

pre-cede
prece-dence
prece-dent
prece-dents
pre-ced·ing

pre-cept
pre-cinct
pre-cincts
pre-cious
pre-cise

pre-cisely
pre-ci-sion
pre-clude
pre-cluded
pre-cludes

pre-clud·ing
pre·cut
prede-ces·sor
prede-ces·sors
pre-de·fined

pre-de·liv-er·ies
pre-de·ter-mined
*pre-dica-ment
predi-cated
pre-dict

pre-dicted
pre-dic·tions
pre-dic·tive
pre-domi-nance
pre-domi-nant

pre-domi-nantly
pre-domi-nates
pre-elec·tion
pre-emi·nence
pre-emi·nent

pre-en-roll-ment
pre-en-trance
pre-ex·ist-ing
pre·fab
*pref-ace

pre-fer
pref-er-able
pref-er-ably
pref-er-ence
pref-er-ences

pre-ferred
*pre-fer-ring
pre-fers
pre-filed
pre-fi-nanc-ing

pre-fit
preg-nancy
pre-hear-ing
pre-holi-day
pre-judge

preju-dice
preju-di-cial
preju-dic-ing
pre-limi-nary
pre-ma-ture

pre-ma-turely
pre-med-ical
pre-miere
prem-ise
prem-ises

pre-mium
pre-mi-ums
pre-nurs-ing
pre-oc-cu-pied
pre-pack-aged

pre-paid
prepa-ra-tion
prepa-ra-tions
pre-pa-ra-tory
pre-pare

pre-pared
pre-pared-ness
pre-par-ers
pre-pares
pre-par-ing

pre-pay
pre-pay-ing
pre-pay-ment
pre-pay-ments
pre-plan-ning

pre-pon-der-ance
pre-pos-ter-ous
pre-print
pre-printed
pre-prints

pre-pro-fes-sional
pre-quali-fi-ca-tion
pre-quali-fied
pre-quali-fy-ing
pre-reg-is-tra-tion

pre-req-ui-site
pre-req-ui-sites
pre-roga-tive
pre-scribe
pre-scribed

pre-scribes
pre-scrib-ing
pre-scrip-tion
pre-scrip-tions
pres-ence

pre-sent, v.
pres-ent, adj. or n.
pre-sen-ta-tion
pre-sen-ta-tions
pre-sented

pre-sent-ing
pres-ently
pre-sents, v.
pres-ents, n.
pres-er-va-tion

pres-er-va-tions
pre-serva-tive
pre-serve
pre-served
pre-serv-ers

pre-serves
pre-serv-ing
presi-dency
presi-dent
presi-den-tial

presi-dents
pre-slung
press
press-board
pressed

presses
press-ing
pres-sure
pres-sured
pres-sures

pres-sur-iz-ing
pres-tige
presto
pre-stressed
pre-sum-ably

pre-sume
pre-sumed
pre-sum-ing
pre-sump-tion
*pre-sump-tu-ous

pre-sup-poses
pre-tend
*pre-tense
*pre-ten-tious
pre-tested

pre-timed
pre-tran-scrip-tion
pret-ties
pretty
pre-vail

pre-vailed
pre-vail-ing
pre-vails
preva-lent
pre-vent

pre-vented
pre-vent-ing
pre-ven-tion
pre-ven-tive
pre-vents

pre-view
pre-vi-ous
pre-vi-ously
pre·war
pre-wired

prey
price
priced
price-less
pricer

prices
pric-ing
prickly
pride
pride-ful

priest
pri·mar-ily
pri·mary
prime
primed

primer
prim-ing
primi-tive
prim-rose
prince

prin-ci·pal
prin-ci-pally
prin-ci-pals
prin-ci-pal-ship
prin-ci·ple

prin-ci-ples
print
printed
printer
print-ers

print-ing
print-ings
prints
print-works
prior

pri-ori-ties
pri-or-ity
prison
pris-oner
pris-on·ers

pris-ons
pri-vacy
pri-vate
pri-vately
privi-lege

privi-leged
privi-leges
prize
prized
prizes

pro
proba-bil-ity
prob-able
prob-ably
pro-bate

probe
probes
prob-lem
prob-lem-at-ical
prob-lems

pro-ce-dure
pro-ce-dures
pro-ceed
pro-ceeded
pro-ceed-ing

pro-ceed-ings
pro-ceeds
pro-cess
pro-cessed
pro-cesses

pro-cess-ing
pro-ces-sion
pro-ces·sor
pro-ces-sors
pro-claim

pro-claimed
*proc-la-ma-tion
pro·cras-ti-na-tion
proc-tor
pro-cure

pro-cured
pro-cure-ment
pro-cure-ments
pro-cur-ing
pro-duce

pro-duced
pro-ducer
pro-duc·ers
pro-duces
pro-duc·ing

pro-duct
pro·duc-tion
pro·duc-tions
pro·duc-tive
pro·duc-tiv·ity

prod-ucts
*pro-fane
*pro-fan·ity
pro-fess
pro·fes-sion

pro·fes-sional
pro·fes-sion-al·ize
pro·fes-sion·ally
pro·fes-sion·als
pro·fes-sions

pro-fes·sor
pro-fes-sors
pro·fi-ciency
pro·fi-cient
*pro-file

pro-files
profit
prof·ita-bil·ity
prof·it-able
prof·it-ably

prof-it·ing
prof-its
pro forma
pro-found
pro-fuse

pro·fu-sion
*prog-no·sis
*prog·nos-ti-ca·tion
pro-gram
pro-grammed

pro-gram-ming
pro-grams
pro-gress
pro-gressed
pro-gresses

pro-gress·ing
pro·gres-sive
pro·gres-sively
pro-hibit
pro·hib-ited

pro·hi-bi-tion
pro·hi-bi-tions
pro·hibi-tive
pro-hib·its
pro-ject, v.

proj-ect, n.
pro-jected
pro-ject·ing
pro-jec-tion
pro-jec-tions

pro-jec·tor
pro-jec·tors
pro-jects, v.
proj-ects, n.
pro-lapse

pro-lapsed
pro-lific
pro-longed
prom
*prome-nade

promi-nence
promi-nent
promi-nently
prom-ise
prom-ised

prom-ises
prom-is·ing
pro-mote
pro-moted
pro-mot·ing

pro·mo-tion
pro·mo-tional
pro·mo-tion-ally
pro·mo-tions
prompt

prompted
prompt-ing
promptly
prompt-ness
prompts

pro·mul-gate
pro·mul-gated
pro·mul-ga-tion
prone
prong

prongs
pro-nounced
proof
proof-ing
proof-read

proofs
propa-ganda
pro-pane
pro·pel
pro-pelled

pro-pel-ler
proper
prop-erly
prop-er-ties
prop-erty

proph-ecy
pro-phetic
pro-po-nents
pro-por-tion
pro-por-tional

pro-por-tion-ate
pro-por-tion-ately
pro-por-tions
pro-posal
pro-pos-als

pro-pose
pro-posed
pro-poses
pro-pos-ing
propo-si-tion

propo-si-tions
pro-prie-tor
pro-prie-tors
pro-prie-tor-ship
pro-pri-ety

props
pro rata
pro-rate
pro-rated
pro-rat-ing

pro-ra-tion
*prose-cute
prose-cut-ing
prose-cu-tion
pros-pect

pro-spec-tive
pros-pects
pro-spec-tus
pros-per-ity
pros-per-ous

pros-tate
pro-tect
pro-tected
pro-tect-ing
pro-tec-tion

pro-tec-tions
pro-tec-tive
pro-tec-tor
pro-tects
pro-tein

pro-teins
pro-test
pro-tested
pro-tests
*pro-to-col

pro-to-type
proud
prouder
proudly
prove

proved
proven
proves
pro-vide
pro-vided

provi-dence
pro-vides
pro-vid-ing
prov-ince
prov-ing

pro-vi-sion
pro-vi-sion-ing
pro-vi-sions
pro-viso
*pro-voca-tive

pro-voked
pro-vok-ing
prox-ies
prox-im-ity
prox-imo

proxy
pru-dent
prune
pry
psy-chi-at-ric

*psy-chia-try
*psy-chic
psy-cho-log-ical
psy-cholo-gist
psy-cholo-gists

psy-chol-ogy
*psy-cho-pathic
pub-lic
pub-li-ca-tion
pub-li-ca-tions

pub-lic-ity
pub-li-cized
pub-li-ciz-ing
pub-licly
pub-lish

pub-lished
pub-lisher
pub-lish-ers
pub-lishes
pub-lish-ing

pud-ding
pud·dle
puff
pull
pulled

pull·ing
pulls
pulp
pulp-ing
pulse

pulses
pump
pumped
pump-ing
pumps

punch
punched
punches
punch-ing
*punc-tu-al·ity

pun-ished
pun·ishes
pun-ish-ment
pupil
pu·pils

pur-chase
pur-chased
pur-chaser
pur-chas·ers
pur-chases

pur-chas·ing
pure
purely
pur·ga-tive
pur·ga-tory

pu·ri-fi-ca-tion
pu·ri-tan
pu·rity
pur·ple
*pur-port

pur-pose
pur-posely
pur-poses
purse
pur-sual

pur-su-ance
pur-su·ant
pur·sue
pur-sued
pur-su·ing

pur-suits
push
push–button
pushed
push-ing

put
pu·trid
puts
put-ting
putty

*puz·zle
puz-zled
pyra-mid
pyra-mided
pyres

py·rome-ters
py·ro-tech·nics

Q

quad-ri-ple·gic
quad-ri-ple-gics
qua-dru-pli-cate
quail
quali-fi-ca-tion

quali-fi-ca-tions
quali-fied
quali-fier
qual-ify
quali-fy·ing

quali-ties
qual-ity
quan-dary
quan-ti-ties
quan-tity

quar-an-tine
*quar-rel-some
quart
quar-ter
*quar-ter-back

quar-terly
quar-ters
quar-tile
quarts
quartz

queen
query
quest
ques-tion
ques-tion-able

ques-tioned
ques-tion·ing
ques-tion-naire
ques-tion-naires
ques-tions

*quib-ble
quick
quicker
quick-est
quickly

quiet
qui-eter
qui-etly
quilt
qui-nine

quit
quit-claim
quite
quits
quiz

quota
quo·tas
quo·ta-tion
quo·ta-tions
quote

quoted
quo-tients
quo-ting

R

rab·bit
rab-bits
race
races
rac·ing

rac-ings
rack
racket
racke-teers
racks

radar
ra·dars
ra·di-at·ing
ra·dia-tion
ra·dia-tor

rad-ical
radio
*ra·dio-ac·tive
ra·dios
ra·dio-tele·phones

rad·ish
ra·dius
raf-ters
raft-ers (persons)
rag·ing

rags
rail
rail-road
rail-road·ing
rail-roads

rails
rail-way
rain
rained
rain-fall

rains
raise
raised
rais-ers
raises

rais-ing
rak·ing
ral-lied
ral-lies
rally

ral-ly·ing
ram-bler
*rami-fi-ca-tion
ramp
ram-pant

ramps
ran
ranch
rancher
ran-che·ros

ranch-ers
ranches
ran·dom
range
rang-ers

ranges
rang-ing
rank
rank-ing
ranks

*ran-sack
rapid
*ra·pid-ity
rap-idly
rap·ids

rap-port
rare
rarely
rash
*rasp-berry

Q

R

rat
rata
rate
rated
rates

rather
*rati-fi-ca-tion
rati-fied
rat-ing
rat-ings

ratio
ra-tion
*ra-tion-al-ize
ra-tion-ing
ra-tios

rat-tle
*rav-en-ous
ra-vine
raw
raw-hide

rayon
razor
re
reach
reached

reaches
reach-ing
re-ac-quainted
react
re-acted

re-ac-tion
re-ac-tion-ary
re-ac-tions
re-ac-tor
re-ac-tors

read
reada-bil-ity
read-able
reader
read-ers

read-ily
readi-ness
read-ing
read-ings
re-ad-just

re-ad-just-ment
reads
ready
re-af-firm
real

re-al-ism
re-al-is-tic
re-al-is-ti-cally
re-ali-ties
re-al-ity

re-ali-za-tion
re-al-ize
re-al-ized
re-al-izing
re-ally

realm
realty
ream-ing
reams
re-ana-lyze

re-ana-lyzed
reap
reap-ing
re-ap-pli-ca-tion
re-ap-point-ment

re-ap-praise
rear
re-ar-ma-ment
re-ar-range
re-ar-range-ment

rea-son
rea-son-able
rea-son-able-ness
rea-son-ably
rea-son-ing

rea-sons
re-as-serts
re-as-sign
re-as-sign-ment
re-as-sure

re-as-sured
re-as-sur-ing
re-bate
re-bounded
re-broad-cast

re-build
re-built
re-but-ted
re-but-ting
re-call

re-call-ing
re-ca-pitu-la-tion
re-capped
re-cap-ping
re-cap-ture

re-ceded
re-ceipt
re-ceipted
re-ceipt-ing
re-ceipts

re·ceiv·able
re·ceiv·ables
re·ceival
re·ceive
re·ceived

re·ceiver
re·ceiv·ers
re·ceiv·er·ship
re·ceives
re·ceiv·ing

re·cent
re·cently
re·cep·tion
re·cep·tion·ist
re·cep·tive

re·cer·ti·fied
re·cess
re·ces·sion
re·charg·ing
re·check

re·checked
re·check·ing
reci·pes
re·cipi·ent
re·cipi·ents

re·cip·ro·cal
re·cip·ro·cate
re·cip·ro·cat·ing
reci·proc·ity
reci·ta·tion

reci·ta·tions
re·cite
reck·less
re·claim
rec·la·ma·tion

re·clas·si·fi·ca·tion
re·clas·si·fi·ca·tions
re·clas·si·fied
re·clas·sify
re·clin·ing

rec·og·ni·tion
rec·og·nize
rec·og·nized
rec·og·nizes
rec·og·niz·ing

rec·ol·lec·tion
rec·om·mend
rec·om·men·da·tion
rec·om·men·da·tions
rec·om·mended

rec·om·mend·ing
rec·om·mends
rec·om·pense
re·com·pres·sion
re·com·pu·ta·tion

rec·on·cile
rec·on·ciled
rec·on·cili·ation
re·con·di·tion
re·con·di·tioned

re·con·di·tion·ing
re·con·nais·sance
re·con·nec·tion
re·con·sid·era·tion
re·con·sid·era·tions

re·con·sid·ered
re·con·sign·ment
re·con·structed
re·con·struc·tion
re·con·struc·tive

re·con·vened
re·con·ven·ing
re·con·ver·sion
re·cord, v.
rec·ord, n.

re·corded
re·corder
re·cord·ers
re·cord·ing
re·cord·ings

re·cords, v.
rec·ords, n.
re·count
re·course
re·cover

re·cov·er·able
re·cov·ered
re·cov·er·ing
re·cov·ers
re·cov·ery

rec·rea·tion
rec·rea·tional
rec·rea·tion·ally
re·cruit
re·cruited

re·cruit·ing
re·cruit·ment
re·cruits
rec·tal
rec·tan·gu·lar

rec·ti·fier
rec·ti·fi·ers
rec·tify
rec·ti·fy·ing
rec·tum

re·cu·per·at·ing
re·cu·pera·tive
recur
re·curred
re·cur·rence

red
red·bud
re·deco·rate
re·deem
re·deema·bility

re·deem-able
re·deemed
re·de-fined
re·demp-tion
re·demp-tions

re·de·pos-it·ing
re·de·sign
re·de·signed
re·de·sign·ing
re·de·vel·op-ment

re·dis·cuss
re·dis·trib-uted
re·doubt
re·dress
re·duce

re·duced
re·ducer
re·duces
re·duc-ing
re·duc-tion

re·duc-tions
re·dun-dant
red-wood
red-woods
reel

re·elected
re·elec-tion
reel-ing
reels
re·em-pha-size

re·em-ploy
re·es-tab-lished
re·evalu-ate
re·evalu-ation
re·ex-am-ine

re·ex-am-ined
refer
*ref-eree
ref-er·eed
ref·er-ence

ref·er-enced
ref·er-ences
ref·er-en-dum
re·fer-ral
re·fer-rals

re·ferred
re·fer-ring
re·fers
re·fig-ure
re·fig-ured

re·fill
re·fills
re·fi-nanc·ing
re·fined
re·fine-ment

re·fin-er·ies
re·fin-ery
re·fines
re·fin-ing
re·fin-ish·ing

re·flect
re·flected
re·flect-ing
re·flec-tion
re·flec-tor

re·flects
re·flux
re·for-es-ta-tion
re·form
re·for-ma-to-ries

re·for-ma-tory
re·frain
re·frained
re·frain-ing
re·fresh

re·fresher
re·fresh-ing
re·fresh-ingly
re·fresh-ments
re·frig-er-ated

re·frig-er-at·ing
re·frig-era-tion
re·frig-era·tor
re·frig-era-tors
ref·uge

re·fund
re·fund-able
re·funded
re·fund-ing
re·funds

re·fusal
re·fuse, v.
ref·use, n.
re·fused
re·fuses

re·fus-ing
re·fute
re·gain
re·gain-ing
regal

*re·ga-lia
re·gard
re·garded
re·gard-ing
re·gard-less

re·gards
re·gen-era·tor
re·gents
*re·gime
*regi-men-ta-tion

re·gion
re·gional
re·gions
reg·is-ter
reg·is-tered

reg·is-ter·ing
reg·is-ters
reg·is-trant
reg·is-trants
reg·is-trar

reg·is-trars
reg·is-tra-tion
reg·is-tra-tions
reg·is-try
reg·let

re·gret
re·gret-fully
re·grets
*re·gret-ta·ble
re·gret-ta·bly

re·gret-ted
re·gret-ting
re·group
regu-lar
regu-larly

regu-lars
regu-late
regu-lated
regu-lat·ing
regu-la-tion

regu-la-tions
regu-la-tors
regu-la-tory
re·ha-bili-tate
re·ha-bili-ta-tion

re·han-dling
re·hang
re·hearsal
re·hearse
re·heat

re·im-burs-able
re·im-burse
re·im-bursed
re·im-burse-ment
re·im-burs·ing

re·in-force
re·in-forced
re·in-force-ment
re·in-force-ments
re·in-forc·ing

re·in-state
re·in-stated
re·in-state-ment
re·in-stat·ing
re·in-sur-ance

re·in-sur-ances
re·in-sured
re·in-surer
re·in-sur·ers
re·in-vested

re·in-vest-ment
re·in-voice
re·is-sue
re·is-sued
re·it-er·ate

re·it-er-ated
re·ject
re·jected
re·ject-ing
re·jec-tion

re·jec-tions
re·jects
re·joice
re·joic-ing
re·kin-dle

re·late
re·lated
re·lates
re·lat-ing
re·la-tion

re·la-tions
re·la-tion-ship
re·la-tion-ships
rela-tive
rela-tively

rela-tives
relax
re·laxa-tion
re·laxed
re·lax-ing

relay
re·layed
re·lay-ers
re·lay-ing
re·lays

re·lease
re·leased
re·leases
re·leas-ing
*re·lent-less

relet
rele-vance
rele-vant
re·lia-bil·ity
re·li-able

re·li-ably
re·li-ance
re·lied
re·lief
re·lieve

re·lieved
re·lieves
re·liev-ing
re·li-gion
re·li-gions

re·li-gious
re·lined
re·lin-quish
re·lin-quished
re·lin-quish-ment

*relish
re·liti-gated
re·load-ing
re·lo-cated
re·lo-cat·ing

re·lo-ca-tion
re·luc-tance
re·luc-tant
rely
re·ly-ing

re·main
re·main-der
re·mained
re·main-ing
re·mains

re·manu-fac-tured
re·manu-fac-turer
re·mark
re·mark-able
re·mark-ably

re·marked
re·marks
re·mar-ried
re·marry
re·me-dial

reme-died
reme-dies
rem·edy
re·mem-ber
re·mem-bered

re·mem-ber-ing
re·mem-bers
re·mem-brance
re·mind
re·minded

re·minder
re·mind-ers
re·mind-ing
re·minds
*remi-nis-cent

re·miss
re·mis-sion
remit
re·mit-tance
re·mit-tances

re·mit-ted
re·mit-ting
*rem-nant
re·model
re·mod-eled

re·mod-el·ing
*re·morse
re·mote
re·mov-able
re·moval

re·move
re·moved
re·mover
re·mov-ers
re·moves

re·mov-ing
re·mu-nera-tion
re·nais-sance
re·named
ren·der

ren-dered
ren-der·ing
ren-ders
*ren·dez-vous
ren·di-tion

re·nege
re·ne-go-ti·ate
re·ne-go-tia-tion
renew
re·newal

re·new-als
re·newed
re·new-ing
re·news
re·nomi-na-tion

re·nounced
re·nounces
reno-vate
reno-vat·ing
reno-va-tion

reno-va-tions
re·nowned
rent
rental
rent-als

rented
rent-ing
rents
re·nun-cia-tion
re·open

re·opened
re·open-ing
re·or-der
re·or-dered
re·or-der·ing

re·orders
re·or-ga-ni-za-tion
re·or-ga-ni-za-tional
re·or-ga-nized
re·pack-aged

re·packed
re·pack-ing
re·paid
re·paint
re·painted

re·paint-ing
re·pair
re·pair-able
re·paired
re·pair-ing

re·pair-men
re·pairs
re·pav-ing
repay
re·pay-able

re·pay-ing
re·pay-ment
re·pay-ments
re·peal
re·pealed

re·peat
re·peated
re·peat-edly
re·peat-ing
re·peats

*repel
*re·pelled
*re·pel-lent
re·per-cus-sions
repe-ti-tion

repe-ti-tions
repe-ti-tious
re·peti-tive
re·place
re·place-able

re·placed
re·place-ment
re·place-ments
re·plac-ing
re·plant-ing

re·plen-ish
rep-lica
rep-li-cas
re·plied
re·plies

reply
re·ply-ing
re·port
re·ported
re·port-edly

re·port-ers
re·port-ing
re·ports
re·pos-sess
re·pos-ses-sion

*rep·re-hen-si·ble
rep·re-sent
rep·re-sen-ta-tion
rep·re-sen-ta-tions
rep·re-sen-ta-tive

rep·re-sen-ta-tives
rep·re-sented
rep·re-sent·ing
rep·re-sents
re·pres-sure

re·pres-sur·ing
*re·prieve
re·print
re·printed
re·print-ing

re·prints
re·pri-sal
re·proach
re·pro-duce
re·pro-duced

re·pro-duc-ible
re·pro-duc·ing
re·pro-duc-tion
re·pro-duc-tions
re·pro-gram-ming

re·pub-lic
re·pub-li·can
re·pu-dia-tion
*re·pul-sive
re·pur-chase

re·pur-chased
repu-ta·ble
repu-ta-tion
re·pute
re·put-edly

re·quest
re·quested
re·quest-ing
re·ques-tion
re·quests

re·quire
re·quired
re·quire-ment
re·quire-ments
re·quires

re·quir-ing
req-ui-site
req-ui-si-tion
req-ui-si-tioned
re·quoted

re·read
re·route
rerun
re·sal-able
re·sale

re·sched-ule
re·sched-uled
re·scind
res·cue
re·search

re·searched
re·searcher
re·searches
re·search-ing
re·seeded

re·seed-ing
re·sell
re·seller
re·sem-blance
re·sent

res·er-va-tion
res·er-va-tions
re·serve
re·served
re·serves

re·serv-ing
re·serv-ist
re·serv-ists
re·ser-voir
re·ser-voirs

reset
re·ship-ping
re·side
resi-dence
resi-dency

resi-dent
resi-den-tial
resi-dents
re·sides
re·sid-ing

re·sid-ual
resi-due
re·sign
res·ig-na-tion
res·ig-na-tions

re·signed
re·signs
resin
res·ins
re·sist

re·sis-tance
re·sis-tant
re·sist-ing
re·sis-tor
re·sis-tors

re·sists
re·so-lici-ta-tion
reso-lutely
reso-lu-tion
reso-lu-tions

re·solve
re·solved
re·solves
re·solv-ing
re·sort

re·sort-ing
re·sound-ing
re·source
re·sources
re·spect

*re·specta-bil·ity
re·spected
re·spect-fully
re·spect-ing
re·spec-tive

re·spec-tively
re·spects
*re·spira-tory
re·spite
re·spond

re·sponded
re·spon-dent
re·spon-dents
re·spond-ing
re·sponse

re·sponses
re·spon-si-bili-ties
re·spon-si-bil·ity
re·spon-si·ble
re·spon-sive

rest
re·state
res·tau-rant
res·tau-rants
rest-less

re·stock-ing
res·to-ra-tion
re·store
re·stored
re·strained

re·straint
re·straints
re·strict
re·stricted
re·stric-tion

re·stric-tions
re·stric-tive
re·stricts
re·strike
rest-rooms

rests
re·sub-mit
re·sub-mit·ted
re·sub-mit-ting
re·sult

re·sult-ant
re·sulted
re·sult-ful
re·sult-ing
re·sults

re·sume
re·sumed
re·sumes
re·sum-ing
re·sump-tion

re·sur-fac·ing
re·sur-vey
re·sus-ci-ta-tion
re·tail
re·tailed

re·tailer
re·tail-ers
re·tail-ing
re·tain
re·tained

re·tain-ing
*re·tali-ate
re·tar-da-tion
re·tarded
re·tard-ing

re·ten-tion
re·tire
re·tired
re·tiree
re·tir-ees

re·tire-ment
re·tir-ing
re·trace-ments
re·tract
*re·trac-tion

re·train-ing
re·treat
re·trieval
re·trieved
re·tro-ac-tive

re·tro-ac-tively
re·tro-spect
re·turn
re·turn-able
re·turned

re·turn-ing
re·turns
re·typ-ing
re·un-ion
re·un-ions

reuse
re·used
re·us-ing
re·valu-ated
re·var-nish·ing

re·veal
re·vealed
re·veal-ing
re·veals
re·vege-ta-tion

reve-la-tion
*re·venge
reve-nue
reve-nues
re·vere

*rev·er·ence
rev·er·end
re·ver·sal
re·ver·sals
re·verse

re·versed
*re·vers·ible
re·vers·ing
re·vert
re·view

re·viewed
re·view·ing
re·views
re·vise
re·vised

re·vis·ing
re·vi·sion
re·vi·sions
re·vi·tal·ize
re·vived

re·vo·ca·ble
re·vo·ca·tion
re·voke
re·vok·ing
revo·lu·tion

revo·lu·tion·ary
re·volver
re·volves
re·volv·ing
revue

re·ward
re·warded
re·ward·ing
re·wards
re·wind

re·wind·ing
re·wired
re·word
re·worded
re·worked

re·work·ing
re·wound
re·write
re·writ·ten
rheu·matic

rho·dium
rib
rib·bon
rib·bons
rice

rich
richer
ride
rider
rides

ridge
*ri·dicu·lous
rid·ing
rife
rifle

rig
right
right·ful
right·fully
rightly

right·ness
right–of–way
rights
rigid
rig·idly

*rig·or·ous
rigs
rim
ring
rings

riot
*ri·ot·ous
ripe
ripen
ripped

rip·ping
rise
risen
rises
ris·ing

risk
risk·ing
risks
risky
rite

*rit·ual
river
riv·er·boat
riv·ers
road

road·bed
roads
roast
roasted
robbed

rob·bery
robe
robot
ro·bust
rock

rocker
rocket
rocks
rocky
rod

rode
*ro·dent
*rodeo
rods
role

roll
roll-back
rolled
roller
roll-ers

roll-ing
rolls
*ro·mance
roof
roof-ing

roofs
room
room-ing
room-mate
rooms

roomy
root
roots
rope
rose

roses
ros·ter
ros-ters
*ros-trum
ro·tary

ro·tat-ing
ro·ta-tion
rouge
rough
rough-ened

rough-en·ing
roughly
*rough-shod
round
round-ing

rounds
roundup
route
routed
route-man

routes
rou-tine
rou-tinely
rou-tines
rout-ing

row
row-boats
rows
royal
roy·al-ties

roy-alty
rub·ber
rub-ber-ize
rub-bing
ru·bies

ruby
rud·der
ru·di-ments
rug
rug·ged

rug-ged-ness
rugs
ru·ined
rule
ruled

rules
rul·ing
rul-ings
ru·mors
run

run-abouts
run–down
run-ning
run·off
run·out

runs
rural
rush
rushed
rust

rus·tic
rust-ing
*rus·tle
rust-proof
rut

*ruth-less
rye

_____

S

sab-bat-ical
sabo-tage
sa·chet
sack
sacks

sa·cral
sa·cred
sac·ri-fice
sac·ri-ficed
sa·crum

sad
sad·dle
sadly
sad-ness
safe

safe-guard
safe-guard·ing
safe-keep·ing
safely
safer

safety
sags
said
sail
sail-boat

sail-ing
sail-ings
saint
saints
sake

sala-bil·ity
salad
sala-ried
sala-ries
sal·ary

sale
sale-able
sales
sales-man
sales-man's

sales-man-ship
sales-men
sales-men's
sales-peo·ple
sales-woman

sa·lient
sa·lin-ity
salmon
*salon
sa·loon

salt
salts
salty
*salu-ta-tion
sa·lute

sal-vage
sal-vaged
sal-va-tion
salves
same

sam·ple
sam-ples
sam-pling
sana-to-rium
*sanc-ti-mo-ni·ous

sanc-tion
sand
sand-blast
sand-pa·per
sands

sand-wich
sandy
san·for-ized
sang
*sani-tar-ium

sani-tary
sani-tiz·ers
*san·ity
sar-dine
sash

sat
sat·el-lites
satin
sat·is-fac-tion
sat·is-fac-to-rily

sat·is-fac-tory
sat·is-fied
sat·is-fies
sat-isfy
sat·is-fy·ing

satu-rate
satu-rated
satu-ra-tion
sau·cer
sauces

*sauer-kraut
sau-sage
sav·age
save
saved

saver
sav·ers
saves
sav·ing
sav-ings

sa·vory
saw
saw-mill
saws
say

say·ing	school	scrim
says	school-ing	script
scale	schools	scripts
scales	sci-ence	scrub
scan	sci-ences	scrub-ber
scan-ner	sci-en-tific	scrub-bing
scan-ning	sci-en-tifi-cally	scrubs
scans	sci-en-tist	scru-pu-lously
*scape-goat	sci-en-tists	scru-tiny
scarce	scis-sors	scuff
scarcely	scope	scurry
scar-ci-ties	scorcher	sea-board
scar-city	score	sea-food
scare	scored	sea-foods
scared	scores	seal
scares	scor-ing	sealed
scar-let	scorn	seal-ing
scars	scotch	seals
scarves	scout	seam
scat-tered	scouts	seamed
scat-ter·ing	scrap	seamer
scene	scrapped	seams
scen-ery	scrap-ping	search
scenes	scraps	searched
sce·nic	scratch	search-ing
scent	scratched	seas
sched-ule	scratch-ing	sea·son
sched-uled	scream	sea·son-able
sched-ules	screen	sea-sonal
sched-ul·ing	screen-ing	sea·son-ally
scheme	screen-ings	sea-soned
schol-ars	screens	sea-sons
schol-ar-ship	screw	seat
schol-ar-ships	screws	seat-ing
scho-las·tic	scribe	seats

sea-way
sec
*se·clu-sion
sec·ond
sec·on-dary

sec-onded
sec-ondly
sec-onds
se·crecy
se·cret

sec·re-tar-ial
sec·re-tar-ies
sec·re-tary
se·crete
se·crets

sec·tari-an·ism
sec-tion
sec-tional
sec-tion-al-iz·ing
sec-tion·als

sec-tioned
sec-tion-ing
sec-tions
sec·tor
sec-tors

secu-lar
se·cure
se·cured
se·cur-ing
se·cu-ri-tics

se·cu-rity
sedan
sedi-ment
sedi-men-ta-tion
see

seed
seeded
seed-ing
seeds
see·ing

seek
seeker
seek-ing
seeks
seem

seemed
seem-ingly
seems
seen
seep

seer-sucker
sees
seg-ment
seg-ments
seg·re-gated

*seg·re-ga-tion
*seis-mo-graph
seize
sel·dom
se·lect

se·lected
se·lect-ing
se·lec-tion
se·lec-tions
se·lec-tive

se·lec-tively
se·lec-tor
se·lec-tors
se·lects
self

self-addressed
self-contained
self-destruction
self-directiveness
self-employed

self-employment
self-evaluation
self-explanatory
self-government
self-help

self-improvement
self-insurance
self-ish
self-laminating
self-protection

self-respect
self-restraint
self-serving
self-starters
self-sufficiency

self-sufficient
self-supporting
self-training
sell
seller

sell-ers
sell-ing
sells
se·mes-ter
se·mes-ters

semi-an·nual
semi-an·nu·ally
semi-monthly
semi-nar
semi-nars

skipped
skips
skull
skunks
sky

sky-line
sky-rocket
sky-rock-et-ing
sky-rock-ets
slab

slabs
slack
slack-ened
slacks
*slan-der-ous

slanted
slate
slated
slats
slaugh-ter

slaugh-tered
sleep
sleeper
sleep-ing
sleeve

sleeves
*slen-der
slice
slick
slicker

slide
slides
slid-ing
slight
slighted

semi-nary	sepa-rate	set
semi-por-no-graphic	sepa-rately	sets
semi-pub-lic	sepa-rat-ing	set-ters
semi-re-tired	sepa-ra-tion	set-ting
semi-re-tire-ment	sepa-ra-tions	set-tle
semi-skilled	sepa-ra-tor	set-tled
semi-trailer	se-pias	set-tle-ment
sen-ate	se-quence	set-tle-ments
sena-tor	se-quences	set-tling
sena-tors	se-quins	setup
send	*se-rene	seven
sender	*se-ren-ity	seven-eighths
send-ing	*ser-geant	sev-en-teen
send-off	se-rial	sev-en-teenth
sends	se-ries	sev-enth
*se-nile	se-ri-ous	sev-en-ties
sen-ior	se-ri-ously	sev-enty
sen-iors	se-ri-ous-ness	seventy-eight
sen-sa-tional	ser-mons	seventy-five
sen-sa-tion-ally	ser-vant	seventy-nine
sense	ser-vants	seventy-six
sensed	serve	seventy-two
senses	served	sev-eral
sen-si-ble	serves	sev-er-al-fold
sens-ing	ser-vice	sev-er-ance
sen-si-tive	ser-vice-able	se-vere
sen-si-tiv-ity	ser-viced	se-verely
sent	ser-vice-man	sew
sen-tence	ser-vice-men	sew-age
sen-ti-ment	ser-vice-men's	sewed
sen-ti-mental	ser-vices	sewer
sen-ti-ments	ser-vic-ing	sew-er-age
*sen-ti-nel	serv-ing	sew-ing
sen-try	ses-sion	sex
sepa-ra-ble	ses-sions	*shabby

shade
shaded
shades
shadow
shaft

shaft-ing
shake
shaker
shak-ers
shall

shal-low
shal-lower
sham-poo
shape
shaped

shapes
shap-ing
share
shared
share-holder

share-hold-ers
share-own-ers
shares
shar-ing
sharp

sharpen
sharp-ened
sharp-ener
sharp-en-ing
sharp-ens

sharp-est
sharply
shat-ter-ing
shave
shaven

shaver
shav-ing
she
shears
sheath-ing

shed
shed-ding
sheds
sheep
sheer

sheet
sheet-ing
sheets
shelf
shell

shel-lac
shells
shel-ter
shel-tered
shelves

shelv-ing
*sher-iff
shield
shield-ing
shift

shifted
shift-ing
shim-ming
shine
shined

shin-gle
shin-gles
shin-ing
shiny
ship

ship-mate
ship-ment
ship-ments
shipped
ship-per

ship-pers
ship-ping
ships
*ship-shape
ship-yard

ship-yards
shirt
shirts
shock
shocked

shoe
shoes
shook
shooks
shoot

shooter
shoot-ing
shop
shopped
shop-per

shop-ping
shops
shop-worn
shore
shores

shore-side
short
short-age
short-ages
shorten

sim·pli-fy·ing
sim·ply
simu-late
simu-lated
si·mul-ta-neous

si·mul-ta-neously
sin
since
sin-cere
sin-cerely

sin-cer·est
sin-cer·ity
sine
sing
sing-ers

sing-ing
sin·gle
sin-gled
sin-gles
sings

sin-gu·lar
sink
sink-ing
sins
sir

sires
sis-sies
sis·ter
sis-ters
sit

site
sites
sits
sit-ting
situ-ate

situ-ated
situ-ation
situ-ations
situs
six

six-teen
six-teenth
sixth
six-ti·eth
six-twelfths

sixty
sixty-one
siz-able
size
sized

sizes
siz-zling
skele-tons
skep-ti·cal
sketch

sketched
sketches
ski
skier
ski·ing

skill
skilled
skil-let
skill-ful
skill-fully

skills
skimpy
skin
skinned
skip

slight-est	small-est	snowed
slightly	small-mouth	snow-fall
slim	smart	so
sling	smarter	soap
slip	smartly	soared
slip-pers	smart-ness	soar-ing
slip-pery	smashed	so·ber-ing
slip-ping	smear	so-called
slips	smear-ing	*so·cia-ble
slither	smears	so·cial
slo·gan	smelter	so·cial-is·tic
slope	smile	so·ciali-za-tion
slopes	smil-ing	so·cial-ized
sloppy	smocks	so·cially
slosh-ing	smoke	so·ci-eties
slot	smok-ers	so·ci-ety
slot-ted	smok-ing	so·cio-eco-nomic
slouch-ing	smooth	so·ci-ol·ogy
*slov-enly	smoother	sock
slow	smoothly	socket
slowed	smudge	sock-ets
slower	smudgy	socks
slow-est	snack	sod
slowly	snacks	soda
slow-ness	snag-ging	sod-ding
sludge	snap	so·dium
sludges	snap-ping	soft
slug	snappy	soft-ball
slug-ging	snaps	soft-ened
*slug-gish	snap-shot	soft-ens
slum	sneak	soil
slum-ber	sneaked	soiled
slump	sneezed	soils
small	*snob-bish	sold
smaller	snow	sol-diers

sole
soled
solely
*sol·emn
soles

so·licit
so·lici-ta-tion
so·lic-ited
so·lic-it-ing
so·lici-tor

so·lici-tors
solid
sol·ids
soli-taires
*soli-tary

solu-bil·ity
sol-uble
so·lu-tion
so·lu-tions
solve

solved
sol-vency
sol-vent
sol-vents
solver

solv-ing
some
some-body
some-day
some-how

some-one
some-place
*som·er-sault
some-thing
some-time

some-times
some-what
some-where
son
song

songs
sonic
son-in-law
sons
soon

sooner
sooth-ing
so·phis-ti-cate
*so·phis-ti-cated
so·phis-ti-ca-tion

sopho-more
sor·did
sorely
sor-ghum
sor-ghums

so·ror-ity
*sor·row
sorry
sort
sorted

sort-ing
sorts
sou
sought
soul

souls
sound
sounder
sound-est
sound-ing

sound-ness
sounds
source
sources
sou·sa-phone

south
south-east
south-east·ern
south-ern
south-west

south-west·ern
sou-ve·nir
soy
soy-bean
soy-beans

spa
space
space-craft
spaced
spacer

spaces
spac-ing
spa-cious
span
span-gled

spare
spared
spare-time
spark
sparked

spar-kle
spar-kling
sparks
speak
speaker

speak-ers
speak-ing
speaks
spear-head·ing
spe-cial

spe·cial-ist
spe·cial-ists
spe·ciali-za-tion
spe·cial-ize
spe·cial-ized

spe·cial-iz·ing
spe-cially
spe-cials
spe·cial-ties
spe-cialty

spe-ci·ate
spe-cies
spe-cific
spe·cifi-cally
speci-fi-ca-tion

speci-fi-ca-tions
spe-cif·ics
speci-fied
speci-fies
spec-ify

speci-fy·ing
speci-men
specs
*spec-ta·cle
spec-tacu·lar

spec-tacu-larly
*spec-ta·tor
spec-ter
spec-trum
specu-la-tion

specu-la-tive
speech
speeches
speed
speed-ing

speed-ome·ter
speeds
speed-way
speedy
spell

spell-bound
spelled
spell-ing
spell-ings
spells

spend
spend-able
spend-ing
spends
spent

sphere
spicer
spikes
spilled
spin-ach

spine
spin-ner
spin-ners
spin-ning
spi·ral

spirit
spir-ited
spir-its
spiri-tual
spite

splash-ing
splen-did
splen-didly
spline
splints

split
split-ting
*splurge
spoke
spo·ken

sponge
spon-sor
spon-sored
spon-sor·ing
spon-sors

spon-sor-ship
*spon-ta-ne·ous
spool
spools
spoons

sport
sport-ing
sports
sports-man-ship
sports-men

spot
spot-lessly
spot-light
spot-lights
spots

spotty
spouse
spouts
sprawled
spray

sprayer	squirt	stamped
spray-ing	stab	*stam-pede
sprays	sta-bil·ity	stamp-ing
spread	sta·bili-za-tion	stamps
spread-ing	sta·bi-lized	stand
spreads	sta·ble	stan-dard
spree	stack	stan-dardi-za-tion
spring	stacked	stan-dard·ize
spring-board	stack-ing	stan-dard-ized
springs	sta-dium	stan-dard-iz·ing
spring-time	staff	stan-dards
sprin-kle	staffed	standby
sprin-kler	staff-ing	stand-ing
sprin-klers	staff-men	stand-ings
sprocket	staffs	stand-pipe
sprock-ets	stage	stand-point
spruce	staged	stand-points
sprue	stages	stands
spur	stain	stand-still
spy-glass	stained	sta·ple
squab-ble	stain-less	sta-pled
squad	stains	sta-pler
*squalid	stair	sta-plers
*squall	stairs	sta-ples
square	stair-way	sta-pling
squarely	stair-ways	star
squares	stake	star-board
squaw	staked	starch
*squawk	stakes	star-ing
*squeam-ish	stak-ing	stars
squeeze	stale-mate	start
squeezes	stal-wart	started
squeez-ing	stal-warts	starter
squir-rel	*stam-ina	start-ers
squir-rels	stamp	start-ing

star-tled
starts
starve
state
stated

stately
state-ment
state-ments
*state-room
states

state-side
states-man-ship
state-wide
static
stat-ing

sta-tion
sta-tion·ary
sta-tioned
sta-tio·ner
sta-tio-ners

sta-tio-nery
sta-tions
sta·tis-ti·cal
stat·is-ti-cian
stat·is-ti-cians

sta·tis-tics
stat-ure
sta·tus
stat-ute
stat-utes

statu-tory
staunch
stay
stayed
stay-ing

stays
stead-fastly
stead-ier
stead-ily
steady

steak
steal-ing
steam
steam-boat
steamed

steamer
steam-ers
steam-ship
steel
steep

steeper
steer-ing
steers
stem
stems

sten-cil
sten-cil·ing
sten-cilled
sten-cils
steno

ste·nog-ra-pher
ste·nog-ra-phers
steno-graphic
ste·nog-raphy
step

step-less
*step-mother
stepped
step-ping
steps

ste·reo
ster-ile
steri-li-za-tion
ster-il-izes
ster-il-iz·ing

ster-ling
*ste·ve-dore
ste·ve-dor·ing
stew-ard
stew-ard·ess

stew-ard-esses
stew-ard-ship
stick
sticker
stick-ers

stick-ing
sticks
stiff
stiff-en·ers
stigma

stile
stiles
still
stills
stimu-lant

stimu-late
stimu-lates
stimu-lat-ing
stimu-la-tion
stimu-la·tors

stimu-lus
stints
sti-pend
stipu-late
stipu-lated

stipu-lates
stipu-lat·ing
stipu-la-tion
stipu-la-tions
stir

stitch
stitched
stitch-ing
stock
stocked

stock-holder
stock-hold·ers
stock-ing
stock-men
stock-pile

stock-piled
stock-piles
stock-pil·ing
stocks
stock-yards

stole
stolen
stom-ach
stomp
stone

stones
stood
stool
stools
stop

stop-gap
stop-over
stop-overs
stopped
stop-per

stop-pers
stop-ping
stops
stor-age
stor-ages

store
stored
store-keeper
store-keep·ers
store-rooms

stores
sto-ries
stor-ing
storm
storms

stormy
story
sto·ry-boards
stove
sto·ver

straight
straighten
straight-ened
straight-en·ing
strain

strainer
strange
strangely
stranger
stran-gu-lat·ing

strap-ping
straps
stra-te·gic
stra·te-gi-cally
strat-egy

*strato-sphere
straw
straw-berry
streaks
stream

streamer
stream-ers
stream-line
stream-lined
stream-liners

streams
street
streets
strength
strengthen

strength-ened
strength-en·ing
strengths
*strenu-ous
*strep-to-coc·cus

strep-to-my·cin
stress
stressed
stresses
stress-ing

stretch
stretched
stretcher
stretch-ers
stricken

strict
strict-est
strictly
stride
strides

strike
strikes
strik-ing
string
strin-gent

string-ers
strings
strip
stripe
striped

stripes
strip-ing
stripped
strip-ping
strips

strive
striv-ing
stroke
strokes
strok-ing

strong
stronger
strong-est
strongly
struck

struc-tural
struc-ture
struc-tured
struc-tures
struc-tur·ing

strug-gle
strug-gling
strut
stub
stub-born

stubs
*stucco
stuck
stu-dent
stu-dents

stud-ied
stud-ies
stu·dio
*stu-di·ous
study

study-ing
stuff
stuffer
stun-ning
stunt

*stu·pen-dous
*stu·por
stur-dier
sturdy
style

styled
styles
styl-ing
styl-ish
sty-mied

sty-rene
*suave
sub-agents
sub-com-mit·tee
sub-com-mit·tees

sub-con-tract
sub-con-trac·tor
sub-con-trac-tors
sub-con-tracts
sub-di-vide

sub-di-vid·ing
sub-di-vi-sion
sub-di-vi-sions
*sub·due
sub-ject

sub-jected
sub-ject·ing
sub-jects
sub-ju-ga-tion
*sub-lease

*sub-lime
sub-ma-rine
sub-ma-rines
sub-merged
sub-mis-sion

sub·mit
sub-mit·tal
sub-mit·ted
sub-mit-ting
*sub-or-di-nate

sub-or-di-nated
sub-para-graph
*sub-poena
sub-ro-ga-tion
sub-scribe

sub-scribed
sub-scriber
sub-scrib·ers
sub-scrib·ing
sub-scrip-tion

sub-scrip-tions
sub-sec-tion
sub-se-quent
sub-se-quently
*sub-side

sub-sidi-ar-ies
sub-sidi-ary
sub-si-dies
sub-sid-ing
sub-si-dize

sub-si-dized
*sub-sidy
sub-sis-tence
sub-stance
sub-stances

sub-stan-dard
sub-stan-tial
sub-stan-tially
sub-stan-ti-ate
sub-stan-ti-ated

sub-stan-ti-ates
sub-stan-tive
sub-stan-tively
sub-sti-tute
sub-sti-tuted

sub-sti-tut-ing
sub-sti-tu-tion
sub-ter-ra-nean
sub-tle
sub-tract

sub-trac-tion
sub-tracts
sub-urb
sub-ur-ban
sub-urbs

sub-ver-sion
*sub-ver-sive
sub-way
sub-zero
suc-ceed

suc-ceeded
suc-ceed-ing
suc-cess
suc-cesses
suc-cess-ful

suc-cess-fully
suc-ces-sion
suc-ces-sive
suc-ces-sively
suc-ces-sor

suc-ces-sors
suc-cumb
such
sucker
suck-ers

suc-tion
sud-den
sud-denly
sue
suedes

suf-fer
suf-fered
suf-ferer
suf-fer-ers
suf-fer-ing

suf-fice
*suf-fi-ciency
suf-fi-cient
suf-fi-ciently
suf-fo-cat-ing

*suf-frage
sugar
sug-gest
sug-gested
sug-gest-ing

sug-ges-tion
sug-ges-tions
sug-gests
sui-cide
suit

suita-bil-ity
suit-able
suite
suited
suites

suit-ing
suits
sul-fide
*sul-len
sul-phite

sul-phur
sum
sum-ma-ries
sum-ma-ri-za-tion
sum-ma-rize

sum-ma-rized
sum-ma-rizes
sum-ma-riz-ing
sum-mary
sum-mer

sum-mers
sum-mer-time
sum-ming
sum-mit
sum-moned

sum-mons
sums
sun
sun-bath-ing
sun-fast

sun-fish
sung
sunny
sun-shine
super

su·perb
su·perbly
su·per-fine
su·per-flu·ous
su·per-im-pose

su·per-in-tend·ency
su·per-in-tend·ent
su·per-in-tend·ents
su·pe-rior
su·pe-ri-or·ity

su·per-mar·ket
su·per-mar-kets
su·per-posed
su·per-sales-man
su·per-sede

su·per-seded
su·per-sedes
su·per-sonic
*su·per-sti-tious
su·per-tank·ers

su·per-vise
su·per-vised
su·per-vis·ing
su·per-vi-sion
su·per-vi·sor

su·per-vi·sors
su·per-vi-sory
sup-plant
sup·ple
sup·ple-ment

sup·ple-mental
sup·ple-men-tary
sup·ple-men-ta-tion
sup·ple-mented
sup·ple-ment·ing

sup·ple-ments
sup-plied
sup-plier
sup-pli·ers
sup-plies

sup·ply
sup·ply·ing
sup-port
sup-ported
sup-porter

sup-port·ers
sup-port·ing
sup-ports
sup-pose
sup-posed

sup·posi-to-ries
*sup-press
supra
*su·prem-acy
su·preme

sur-charge
sure
surely
sur·est
sure-ties

sur-face
sur-faced
sur-faces
sur-fac·ing
surf-ing

surge
sur-geon
sur-geons
sur-gery
sur-gi·cal

surg-ing
*sur-mise
*sur-mount
sur-mounted
sur-passed

sur-passes
sur-plus
sur-pluses
sur-prise
sur-prised

sur-prises
sur-pris·ing
sur-pris-ingly
sur-ren·der
sur-ren-dered

sur-ren-der·ing
sur-ren-ders
sur-round
sur-round·ing
sur-round-ings

sur·tax
*sur-veil-lance
sur·vey
sur-veyed
sur-veyor

sur-vey·ors
sur-veys
sur-vival
sur-vive
sur-vived

sur-viv-ing
sur-vivor
sur-vi-vors
sur-vi-vor-ship
*sus-cep-ti-ble

sus-pect
sus-pect-ing
sus-pend
sus-pended
sus-pend-ing

sus-pense
sus-pen-sion
*sus-pi-cion
*sus-pi-cious
sus-tain

sus-tain-able
sus-tained
sus-tain-ing
*sus-te-nance
swal-low

swamp
swamped
swamps
swan
swap

swatch
swatched
swatches
swear
swear-ing

sweat
sweater
sweat-ers
sweep
sweep-ers

sweep-ing
sweeps
sweet
sweet-en-ers
swell

swift
swim
swim-ming
swine
swing

swinger
swings
switch
switch-board
switched

switches
switch-ing
swivel
*swoop
sworn

syca-more
*syl-la-ble
sym-bol
sym-bolic
sym-bol-ism

sym-bols
sym-pa-thetic
sym-pa-thize
sym-pa-thy
sym-phony

sym-po-sia
*sym-po-sium
symp-toms
syn-di-cate
syn-di-cated

*syno-nym
syn-the-sis
*syn-the-size
syn-thetic
syn-thet-ics

syrup
sys-tem
sys-tem-atic
sys-tem-ati-cally
*sys-tema-tize

sys-tems

T

tab
table
ta-bled
ta-bles
ta-ble-spoon

tab-let
ta-ble-tops
tab-lets
ta-ble-ware
*taboo

tabs
tabu-late
tabu-lates
tabu-lat-ing
tabu-la-tion

tabu-la-tions
tabu-la-tor
ta-chome-ter
tacked
tackle

tack-led
tack-ling
tact
*tact-ful
tac-ti-cal

tac-tics
taf-feta
tag
tags
tail

tailed
tai-lor
tai-lored
take
taken

take–over
taker
tak-ers
takes
tak-ing

tal-ent
tal-ents
talk
talked
talk-ing

talks
tall
tally
tamely
tamp

tamp-ing
tan
tan-dem
*tan-gent
tan-gi-ble

tan-gled
tank
tank-age
tanker
tank-ers

tanks
*tan-ta-mount
tap
tape
taped

ta-pered
tapes
tap-ing
tap-ings
tapped

tap-ping
tar
tar-di-ness
tardy
tar-get

tar-iff
tar-iffs
tarry
task
tasks

taste
tastes
tast-ing
tat-too-ing
taught

tav-ern
tax
taxa-bil-ity
tax-able
taxa-tion

taxed
taxes
taxi
taxi-cab
tax-ied

tax-ing
tax-payer
tax-pay-ers
tax-pay-ing
tea

teach
teacher
teach-ers
teaches
teach-ing

team
teams
team-work
tear
tear-ing

tears
tear-sheet
tea-spoon
tech-nic
tech-ni-cal

tech-ni-cali-ties
tech-ni-cal-ity
tech-ni-cally
tech-ni-cian
tech-ni-cians

tech-nique
tech-niques
tech-nolo-gist
tech-nolo-gists
tech-nol-ogy

T

te·di·ous
teen
teen–age
teen–agers
teens

teeth
*tee·to·taler
tele-com-mu-ni-ca-tions
tele-gram
tele-grams

tele-graph
tele-graphic
tele-me-ter·ing
*te·lepa-thy
tele-phone

tele-phoned
tele-phones
tele-phon·ing
tele-scope
tele-scop·ing

tele-type
tele-vi-sion
tele-vi-sions
tell
tell-ers

tell-ing
tells
tel·lu-rium
tem·per
tem·pera-ment

tem·pera-men-tal
*tem-per·ate
tem·pera-ture
tem·pera-tures
tem-pered

tem-pers
tem-pest
tem-plates
tempo
tem·po-rar·ily

tem·po-rary
tempt
temp-ta-tion
ten
te·na-cious

te·na-ciously
*te·nac-ity
ten-ancy
ten·ant
ten-ants

tend
tended
ten·den-cies
ten-dency
tender, n.

ten·der, v.
ten-dered
ten-ders
tend-ing
tends

*tene-ment
ten·nis
tens
tense
ten-sile

ten-sion
tent
ten·ta-tive
ten·ta-tively
tenth

tents
ten·ure
term
termed
ter·mi-nal

ter·mi-nals
ter·mi-nate
ter·mi-nated
ter·mi-nates
ter·mi-na-tion

ter·mi-na-tions
ter·mi-nol·ogy
ter-mite
ter-mites
terms

ter-race
ter-rain
ter-ri·ble
ter-ri·bly
ter-rific

ter·ri-fied
ter·ri-to-rial
ter·ri-to-ries
ter·ri-tory
*terse

test
tested
tester
tes·ti-cle
tes·ti-fied

tes·tify
tes·ti-fy·ing
tes·ti-mo-nial
tes·ti-mo-ni·als
tes·ti-mo-nies

tes·ti·mony
test-ing
test-ings
tests
text

text-book
text-books
tex-tile
tex-tiles
texts

tex-ture
tex-tured
tex-tures
tex-tur·ing
than

thank
thank-ful
thank-ing
thanks
that

that's
the
thea-ter
thea-ters
the·at-ri·cal

theft
thefts
their
theirs
them

theme
them-selves
then
thence
thence-forth

the-ol·ogy
theo-ret-ical
theo-reti-cally
theo-ries
theory

thera-pist
thera-pists
ther-apy
there
there-abouts

there-af·ter
thereat
thereby
there-fore
there-from

therein
there'll
thereof
thereon
there's

thereto
there-with
ther-mal
ther·mo-cou-ples
ther-mome-ters

ther-mo-stat
ther-mo-stats
these
the·sis
they

they'll
they're
they've
thick
thick-ness

thick-nesses
thief
thiev-ery
thin
thing

things
think
think-ers
think-ing
thinks

thin-ner
third
thirdly
thirds
thir-teen

thir-ties
thirty
thirty–eight
thirty–first
thirty–five

thirty–four
thirty–nine
thirty–one
thirty–seventh
thirty–six

thirty–two
this
this-tle
thor-ough
thor·ough-bred

thor-oughly
those
though
thought
thought-ful

thought-fully
thought-ful-ness
thoughts
thou-sand
thou-sands

thrall
thrash-ing
thread-ing
threads
threat

threaten
threat-ened
threat-en-ing
threats
three

three-eighths
three-fourths
three-quarters
three-sixteenths
three-some

three-twelfths
thresh-old
threw
thrift
thrifty

thrill
thrilled
thrill-ing
thrips
thrives

thriv-ing
throat
throb-bing
throt-tle
through

through-out
throw
throw-ing
thrown
throws

thus
thy-roid-ec-tomy
tick
ticket
tick-et-ing

tick-ets
tick-ler
ticks
tidal
tie

tied
tie-in
tier
ties
tie-up

tight
tight-en-ing
tighter
tightly
tile

tiled
till
tilt
tim-ber
time

timed
time-li-ness
timely
timer
times

time-saver
time-sav-ing
time-ta-ble
*ti-mid-ity
tim-ing

tin
ti-ni-est
tin-ker
tin-plate
tins

tint
tints
tiny
tip
tipped

tips
tire
tired
tire-lessly
tires

*tire-some
tir-ing
tis
tis-sue
tis-sues

ti-ta-nium
tithe
tith-ers
title
ti-tled

ti-tles
to
toast
toaster
toast-mas-ters

to·bacco	tool	tough
today	tooled	tougher
to·day's	tool-ing	tour
toe	tools	tour-ing
toes	tooth	tour-ist
to·gether	top	tour-ists
to·geth-ers	top-coats	tour-na-ment
toil	topic	tour-na-ments
token	top·ics	tour-ney
told	top=notch	tours
tol·er-ance	topo-graphi-cally	to·ward
tol·er-ances	to·pog-raphy	to·wards
tol-er·ant	topped	tow·els
tol-er·ate	top-pling	tower
tol·er-ated	tops	tow·ers
toll	*topsy=turvy	town
*toll-gate	top-work	towns
tolls	top-work·ing	town-ship
to·mato	torch	town-ships
to·ma-toes	*tor-ment	toxic
to·mor-row	tor-nado	toxin
to·mor-rows	tor-na-does	toy
ton	to·roids	toys
tonal	torque	trace
tone	*tor·rid	traced
tones	*tor-ture	tracer
tongue	total	trac-ing
to·night	to·taled	track
ton-nage	to·tal-ing	track-age
tons	to·tally	tracks
ton·sil	to·tals	tract
ton·sil-lec-tomy	touch	trac-tion
ton-sils	*touch-down	trac-tor
too	touched	trac-tors
took	touch-ing	tracts

trade	trans	trans-la-tions
traded	trans-act	*trans-lu-cent
trade-mark	trans-acted	trans-mis-sion
trade-marked	trans-ac-tion	trans-mit
trade-marks	trans-ac-tions	trans-mit·tal
trad-ers	trans-at-lan-tic	trans-mit·ted
trades	trans-con-ti-nen-tal	trans-mit·ter
trades-peo·ple	tran-scribe	trans-mit-ting
trad-ing	tran-scribed	trans-pa-cific
tra·di-tion	tran-scrib·ers	trans-par-en-cies
tra·di-tional	tran-scrib·ing	trans-par-ency
tra·di-tion-ally	tran-script	trans-par·ent
tra·di-tions	tran-scrip-tion	tran-spired
traf-fic	tran-scripts	tran-spir·ing
trage-dies	trans-fer	*trans-plant
trag-edy	trans-feree	trans-port
tragic	trans-ferred	trans-por-ta-tion
trail	trans-fer-ring	trans-ported
trailer	trans-fers	trans-port·ing
trail-ers	trans-form	trans-ports
train	trans-formed	trans-versely
trained	trans-former	trap
trainee	trans-form·ers	trapped
train-ees	trans-fu-sion	trap-ping
train·ee-ships	trans-fu-sions	trash
trainer	tran-sient	trau-matic
train-ing	tran-sis·tor	travel
trains	tran-sis-tor-ized	trav-eled
trait	tran-sis-tors	trav-el·ers
*trai-tor	tran-sit	trav-el·ing
traits	tran-si-tion	trav-els
tramp	tran-si-tional	tra-verses
*tram-ple	*trans-late	*trav-esty
*tran-quil	trans-lat·ing	trawl-ers
*tran-quil-lity	trans-la-tion	tray

trays
*treach-er·ous
trea-son
trea-sure
trea-sured

trea-surer
trea-sur·ers
trea-sures
trea-sury
trea-sury's

treat
treated
trea-ties
treat-ing
*trea-tise

treat-ment
treat-ments
treats
treaty
tre-bled

tree
trees
trem-bling
tre·men-dous
tre·men-dously

tremor
trench
trend
trends
trial

tri·als
tri-an·gle
*tri-an-gu·lar
tribal
tribu-la-tions

tribu-tar·ies
trib-ute
trickle
tri-color
tried

tries
tri·fle
trig-ger
trigo-nome·try
*tril-lion

trim
trimmed
trim-ming
trio
trip

tri·ple
tri-pled
trip-li-cate
trips
tri·pur-pose

tri-umph
*tri·um-phant
*triv-ial
trol-ley
trooper

troop-ers
troops
tro-phies
trop-ical
trot-lines

trou-ble
trou-bled
trou-bles
trou·ble-shoot·ing
troughs

trou-sers
trout
trowel
*tru·ant
truck

truck-ers
truck-ing
truck-load
trucks
true

*tru·ism
truly
trum-pet
trusses
trust

trustee
trust-ees
trust-ing
trusts
trust-wor·thy

trusty
truth
truth-ful
truth-fully
try

try·ing
tub
tube
tu·ber-cu-lo·sis
tubes

tub·ing
tu·bu-lar
tui-tion
tulip
tum-bler

tum-blers
tuna
tune
tune-up
*tung-sten

tun-nel
tun-nels
tur-bine
tur-bo-charger
tur-bu-lent

tur-key
tur-keys
tur-moil
tur-moils
turn

turned
turn-ing
tur-nip
turn-out
turn-outs

turn-over
turn-overs
*turn-pike
turns
turn-ta-ble

tur-pen-tine
twain
twelfth
twelve
twen-ties

twen-ti-eth
twenty
twenty-first
twenty-five
twenty-four

twenty-nine
twenty-seven
twenty-third
twenty-three
twenty-two

twice
twi-light
twin
twine
twinge

twins
twist
two
two-fifths
two-thirds

tying
type
typed
typer
types

type-writer
type-writ-ers
type-writ-ing
type-writ-ten
typ-ical

typ-ing
typ-ist
typ-ists
ty-po-graph-ical
*ty-ran-ni-cal

*ty-rant

U

ubiq-uity
ugly
ulcer
ul-ti-mate
ul-ti-mately

*ul-ti-ma-tum
ultra
um-bil-ical
*um-pire
un-able

un-ac-cept-able
*un-ac-count-able
un-ac-cred-ited
*un-ac-cus-tomed
un-ac-knowl-edge

un-af-fected
un-afraid
un-al-lo-cated
un-al-ter-ably
*una-nim-ity

unani-mous
unani-mously
un-an-swered
un-ap-proved
un-as-sem-bled

un-at-trac-tive
un-au-tho-rized
un-availa-bil-ity
un-avail-able
un-avoid-able

un·avoid-ably
un·bal-anced
un·beat-able
un·be-liev-able
un·be-liev-ably

un·bi-ased
un·canny
un·cer-tain
un·cer-tain-ties
un·cer-tainty

un·chal-lenged
un·changed
un·checked
uncle
un·clear

un·clut-tered
un·col-lected
*un·com-fort-able
un·com-mit-ted
un·com-pressed

*un·con-cerned
un·con-di-tional
un·con-di-tion-ally
*un·con-scious
un·con-tra-dicted

un·con-trol-la·ble
un·con-trolled
un·co-op-era-tive
un·cover
un·cov-ered

un·crate
un·da-ted
un·de-liv-er-able
un·de-liv-ered
*un·de-ni-able

un·de-pend-able
under
un·der-charge
un·der-cut
un·der-de·vel·oped

un·der-em·ploy·ment
un·dergo
un·der-goes
un·der-go·ing
un·der-gone

un·der-gradu·ate
un·der-gradu·ates
un·der-ground
*un·der-handed
un·der-lies

un·der-line
un·der-lined
un·der-lin·ing
un·der-ly·ing
*un·der-mine

un·der-neath
*un·der-rate
un·der-score
un·der-signed
un·der-sized

un·der-stand
un·der-stand·able
un·der-stand·ably
un·der-stand·ing
un·der-stands

un·der-stood
un·der-take
un·der-taken
*un·der-taker
un·der-takes

un·der-tak·ing
un·der-tak·ings
un·der-took
un·der-way
un·der-write

un·der-writer
un·der-writ·ers
un·der-writ·ing
un·der-writ·ten
un·de-sir-able

un·de-tected
un·dis-trib-uted
un·dis-turbed
un·di-vided
un·do-ing

un·doubt-edly
undue
un·duly
un·earned
*un·easi-ness

*un·easy
un·em-ploy-able
un·em-ploy-ables
un·em-ployed
un·em-ploy-ment

un·en-force-able
*un·equal
un·even
un·ex-celled
un·ex-pect-edly

un·ex-pended
un·fail-ing
un·fair
un·fa-mil-iar
un·fa-vor-able

U

un·filled
un·fin·ished
un·fold
un·fold·ing
un·fore·see·able

un·fore·seen
*un·for·get·ta·ble
un·for·tu·nate
un·for·tu·nately
un·fused

*un·godly
un·gummed
un·hap·pily
un·hap·pi·ness
un·happy

*un·healthy
un·heard
un·hesi·tat·ingly
un·hon·ored
uni·cel·lu·lar

un·iden·ti·fied
uni·fi·ca·tion
uni·fied
uni·form
uni·for·mity

uni·forms
*unify
*un·im·proved
un·in·sured
un·in·tel·li·gi·ble

un·in·ter·ested
un·in·ter·rupted
union
union·ized
unions

unique
uniquely
*uni·son
unit
unite

united
unit·ized
units
*unity
uni·ver·sal

uni·ver·sally
*uni·verse
uni·ver·si·ties
uni·ver·sity
un·just

un·jus·ti·fi·ably
*un·kempt
un·known
un·law·ful
un·less

un·like
un·likely
un·lim·ited
un·load
un·loaded

un·loader
un·load·ing
*un·man·age·able
un·mar·ried
un·matched

un·mis·tak·ably
*un·natu·ral
un·nec·es·sar·ily
un·nec·es·sary
un·needed

un·ob·li·gated
un·ob·tain·able
*un·oc·cu·pied
un·of·fi·cially
un·opened

un·op·posed
un·or·tho·dox
un·pack
un·pack·ing
un·paid

un·par·al·leled
un·par·don·able
un·pleas·ant
un·prece·dented
un·pre·dict·able

*un·pre·medi·tated
un·pre·pared
*un·prof·it·able
un·pro·tected
un·proven

un·quali·fied
un·quali·fiedly
un·ques·tion·ably
un·ques·tioned
un·re·al·is·tic

un·rea·son·able
un·rea·son·ably
un·re·lated
un·re·leased
un·re·serv·edly

un·rest
un·re·stricted
un·ruly
un·sal·able
un·sat·is·fac·tory

un·scru-pu-lous
un·sealed
un·se-cured
*un·seemly
un·self-ish

un·set-tled
un·set-tling
un·shipped
un·skilled
un·so-lic-ited

un·sound
un·sub-scribed
un·sub-si-dized
un·suc-cess·ful
un·sur-passed

un·taxed
un·ten-able
until
un·timely
un·tir-ing

unto
*un·told
un·trained
un·trimmed
un·turned

un·tu-tored
un·us-able
un·used
un·usual
un·usu-ally

un·uti-lized
un·wanted
un·wel-come
un·will-ing
un·will-ing-ness

un·wise
un·wit-tingly
un·work-able
*un·wor-thy
un·wrap

un·writ-ten
up
up·com-ing
up·date
up·dated

up·dates
up·dat-ing
up·grade
up·graded
up·grad-ing

up·heaval
up·held
up·hold-ing
up·holds
up·hol-stered

up·hol-ster-ing
up·hol-stery
up·keep
up·land
up·lands

upon
upper
up·pers
*up·right
up·roars

ups
upset
up·stairs
up·stream
up·surge

up·turns
up·ward
up·wards
*ura-nium
urban

urge
urged
ur·gency
ur·gent
ur·gently

urges
urg·ing
uri-naly·sis
uri-nary
urine

urolo-gists
us
us·able
usage
use

used
use·ful
use-fully
use·ful-ness
use-less

user
users
uses
usher
using

usual
usu-ally
*usurp
uten-sils
*utili-tar·ian

utili-ties
util-ity
uti-li-za-tion
uti-lize
uti-lized

uti-lizes
uti-liz-ing
ut-most
*ut-ter-ance
ut-ter-ing

V

va-can-cies
va-cancy
va-cant
*va-cate
va-cat-ing

va-ca-tion
va-ca-tion-ist
va-ca-tion-ists
va-ca-tions
*vac-ci-na-tion

*vac-cine
vacuum
vacu-ums
vague
vaguely

vain
*val-en-tine
*valet
valid
*vali-date

vali-dated
vali-da-tion
va-lidi-ties
va-lid-ity
val-ley

val-leys
valor
valu-able
valu-ables
valu-ation

valu-ations
value
val-ued
val-ues
valve

valves
van
van-dal-ism
*va-nilla
van-ish

*van-ity
vans
vapor
va-quero
vari-able

vari-ables
vari-ance
vari-ances
vari-ation
vari-ations

var-ied
var-ies
va-rie-ties
va-riety
vari-ous

vari-ously
var-nish
var-nishes
var-sity
vary

vary-ing
vast
vastly
vault
vaults

vege-ta-ble
vege-ta-bles
*vege-tar-ian
vege-ta-tion
*ve-he-ment

ve-hi-cle
ve-hi-cles
ve-loc-ity
vel-vety
vend

ven-dor
ven-dors
*ve-neer
*ven-er-able
ve-ne-tian

*venge-ance
*veni-son
vent
vented
ven-ti-lat-ing

ven-ti-la-tion
ven-ti-la-tor
ven-ti-la-tors
vents
ven-ture

ven-tured
*ve·rac-ity
ver·bal
ver-bally
ver-ba·tim

veri-fi-ca-tion
veri-fied
veri-fier
veri-fies
ver·ify

veri-fying
*veri-table
*ver-nacu·lar
ver·sa-tile
ver·sa-til·ity

versed
ver-sion
ver-sions
ver·sus
ver-ti·cal

ver·ti-cally
very
ves·per
ves·sel
ves-sels

vest
vested
ves·ti-bule
vest-ing
vest-ments

vests
vet-eran
vet-er·ans
vet·eri-nar·ian
vet·eri-nary

veto
vex·ing
via
vi·able
*vi·bra-tion

*vi·cari-ous
vice
vi·cini-ties
vi·cin-ity
vi·cious

vic·tim
vic·tim-ized
vic-tims
*vic·to-ri·ous
vic-tory

view
viewed
viewer
view-ing
view-point

view-points
views
vigi-lance
*vigi-lant
vigor

vig-or·ous
vig-or-ously
villa
vil-lage
vil-lages

vim
*vin·di-ca-tion
*vin·dica-tive
*vine-gar
vine-yards

vin-tage
vinyl
vi·nyls
vio-late
vio-lat·ing

vio-la-tion
vio·la-tions
vio·la·tor
vio·la-tors
vio-lence

vio-lent
vio-let
vir·gin
vir·tu-ally
vir·tue

vir-tues
virus
visa
vis-come-ters
vis-cos·ity

visi-bil·ity
vis-ible
vi·sion
visit
visi-ta-tion

vis-ited
vis-it·ing
visi-tor
visi-tors
vis·its

vis·ors
vista
vi·sual
vi·su-al·ize
vi·su-ally

vitae
vital
vi·tal·ity
vi·tal·iz·ing
vi·tally

vi·ta-min
vi·ta-mins
vi·ti-ated
*vi·va·cious
vivid

vo·cabu·lary
vocal
vo·ca·tion
vo·ca·tional
*vo·cif-er·ous

voice
voices
void
vola-tile
*vo·li-tion

volt
volt-age
volts
vol-ume
vol-umes

*vo·lu·mi·nous
vol·un·tar·ily
vol·un·tary
vol·un·teer
vo·ra·cious

vote
voted
vot·ers
votes
vot·ing

vouched
voucher
vouch-ers
*voy·age
*vul·ner-able

W

wage
waged
*wager
wages
wagon

waist
wait
waited
wait-ing
waive

waived
waiver
waiv-ers
waiv-ing
wake

walk
walked
walkie
walk-ing
walk-outs

walks
walk-ways
wall
wall-board
walled

wal·let
wal-lets
wal-lops
wall-pa·per
walls

wal·nut
wan-der
wan-der·ers
wan-der·ing
wan-ders

want
wanted
want-ing
wants
war

ward
war·den
ward-robe
wards
ware-house

ware-house-man's
ware-house-men
ware-house·men's
ware-houses
ware-hous·ing

ware-rooms
war-fare
warm
warm-est
warmly

warmth
warned
warn-ing
warn-ings
warns

*warp
war-rant
war-ranted
war-rant·ing
war-rants

war-ranty
wars
war-ship
war-ships
war-time

was
wash
wash-able
washed
washer

wash-ers
wash-ing
wash-room
wasn't
waste

waste-bas·ket
wasted
waste-ful
wast-ing
watch

watched
watches
watch-ing
watch-mak·ers
water

wa·ter-borne
wa·terer
wa·ter-ers
wa·ter-flow
wa·ter-fowl

wa·ter-ing
wa·ter-melon
wa·ter-mel·ons
wa·ter-proof
wa·ters

wa·ter-shed
wa·ter-tight
wa·ter-way
wa·ter-ways
wa·ter-works

watt
watt-age
watts
wave
wax

waxed
waxes
wax·ing
way
way-bill

way-billed
ways
way-side
we
weak

weak-ened
weak-ens
weaker
weak-ness
weak-nesses

wealth
weapon
weap-ons
wear
wear-ing

*wea·ri-some
wears
weary
weather
weath-ered

weave
weav-ing
web
web-bing
web-bings

we'd
wed
wed-dings
wedge
wedges

*wed-lock
wee
weed
weeds
week

week-day
week-end
week-end·ers
week-ends
weekly

weeks
weigh
weighed
weigh-ing
weighs

weight
weighted
weight-ing
weights
*weird

W

wel-come
wel-comed
wel-comes
wel-com·ing
welded

welder
weld-ing
wel-fare
we'll
well

well-being
wells
welted
went
we're

were
weren't
west
west-erly
west-ern

west-erner
wests
west-ward
wet
wet-ta·ble

we've
whale
wharf
wharf-age
what

what-ever
what's
what-so-ever
wheat
wheel

wheel-bar·row
wheeled
wheeler
wheel-ing
wheels

when
when-ever
where
where-abouts
whereas

whereby
where-fore
wherein
whereof
where-upon

wher-ever
whether
whew
which
which-ever

while
whims
*whim-si·cal
whip-ping
whis-key

whis-tle
whis-tles
whis-tling
white
white-wall

whit-tles
who
who-ever
whole
whole-hearted

whole-heart·edly
whole-sale
whole-saler
whole-sal·ers
whole-sales

whole-sal·ing
whole-some
who'll
wholly
whom

*whoop
who's
whose
who've
why

wick
wide
widely
widen
wid-ened

wid-en·ing
wider
wide-spread
wid·est
widow

wid·ows
width
widths
*wield
wife

wife's
wig
wig·gle
wig·wag
wild

wild-cat
wild-est
wild-life
wiles
will

will-fully
will-ing
will-ingly
will-ing-ness
win

wind
wind-fall
win-dow
win-dows
wind-storm

wine
win-ery
wines
wing
wings

win-ner
win-ners
win-ning
win-nings
wins

win-ter
win-ters
win-try
wipe
wiper

wipes
wire
wired
wires
wir-ing

wis-dom
wise
wisely
wish
wished

wishes
wish-ful
wish-ing
wit
witch

with
with-draw
with-draw-able
with-drawal
with-draw-als

with-draw-ing
with-drawn
with-draws
wither
with-held

with-hold
with-hold-ing
within
with-out
with-stand

wit-ness
wit-nessed
wit-nesses
*wit-ti-cism
wives

woe-ful
woman
wom-an's
women
wom-en's

won
won-der
won-dered
won-der-ful
won-der-fully

won-der-ing
won-der-land
won-ders
won't
wood

wooded
wooden
wood-land
wood-lands
woods

wood-stock
woodsy
wood-work
wood-work-ing
woody

wool
word
worded
word-ing
words

wore
work
work-able
worka-day
work-book

worked
worker
work-ers
work-ing
work-ings

work-load
work-man-like
work-man's
work-man-ship
work-men

work-men's
works
work-sheets
work-shop
work-shops

workup
world
worlds
world-wide
wormed

worn
wor-ried
wor-ries
wor·ri-some
worry

worse
wor-ship
worst
wor-sted
wor-steds

worth
worth-while
wor·thy
would
wouldn't

wound
wounded
woven
wran-gler
wrap

wrapped
wrap-per
wrap-ping
wrap-pings
wraps

*wrath-ful
wreath
wreck
wrecked
wrecks

wrench
wrenches
wres-tling
*wretched
wring-ers

wrin-kle
wrin-kles
wrist
write
writer

writ-ers
writes
write-up
writ-ing
writ-ings

writ-ten
wrong
wrong-ful
wrongly
wrote

wrought
wryly

X

x-ray
x-rays

Y

yacht
yachts-men
yard
yard-age
yards

yard-sticks
yarn
yarns
ye
yeah

year
year-book
year-books
yearly
*yearn

year-round
years
yel·low
yes
yes-ter-day

yes-ter-days
yet
yield
yielded
yield-ing

yields
you
you'd
you'll
young

younger
young-ster
young-sters
your
you're

yours
your-self
your-selves
youth
youth-ful

you've
yule-tide

zone
zoned
zones
zon·ing
zoom-ing

zoos

Z

zag
zero
ze·roed
zest
zig

*zig·zag
zinc
zip
zip-pers
zippy